U.S. IMMIGRATION POLICY
AND THE UNDOCUMENTED

U.S. IMMIGRATION POLICY AND THE UNDOCUMENTED

Ambivalent Laws, Furtive Lives

Helene Hayes

Foreword by Eric R. Kingson

Westport, Connecticut
London

Library of Congress Cataloging-in-Publication Data

Hayes, Helene, 1940–
    U.S. immigration policy and the undocumented : ambivalent laws, furtive lives /
Helene Hayes ; foreword by Eric R. Kingson.
      p.   cm.
    Includes bibliographical references and index.
    ISBN 0–275–95410–2 (alk. paper)—ISBN 0–275–95411–0 (pbk. : alk. paper)
    1. Illegal aliens—Government policy—United States.   2. United States—Emigration and
immigration—Government policy.   3. United States. Immigration Reform and Control Act
of 1986.   I. Title.
    JV6483.H383   2001
    323.6′31—dc21   00–069274

British Library Cataloguing in Publication Data is available.

Library of Congress Catalog Card Number: 00–069274
ISBN 0–275–95410–2
    0–275–95411–0 (pbk.)

First published in 2001

Praeger Publishers, 88 Post Road West, Westport, CT 06881
An imprint of Greenwood Publishing Group, Inc.
www.praeger.com

Printed in the United States of America

The paper used in this book complies with the
Permanent Paper Standard issued by the National
Information Standards Organization (Z39.48–1984).

10 9 8 7 6 5 4 3 2 1

To my Irish immigrant parents
John Hayes and Helena O'Brien Hayes
Who taught me to love two countries

Contents

Tables and Figures

TABLES

FIGURES

Foreword

Eric R. Kingson

Helene Hayes, the daughter of Irish immigrants and a sister of the Good Shepherd, writes eloquently about immigration reforms run amiss.

The 1986 Immigration Reform and Control Act (IRCA) was implemented with the twin goals of normalizing the lives of long-term undocumented persons while simultaneously discouraging others from entering the United States. An amnesty provision offered legal status to a select group of the long-term undocumented. Sanctions were implemented for employers hiring undocumented. Yet, fifteen years later, the undocumented population is larger and the politics of immigration reform increasingly divisive. What went wrong? What remains to be done?

Those interested in fashioning the next round of immigration reforms will benefit from reading Dr. Hayes's story of what went wrong. They will benefit from her thoughtful analysis of how, in spite of what were often the best of intentions, the legislative compromises and complexities of implementation conspired to create many negative and unintended consequences for the nation and for a highly vulnerable and often exploited group of people. They will benefit from Hayes's careful research, including first-hand stories, which provide rare insight into the lives of undocumented persons.

This book is based on research Dr. Hayes conducted into the lives of Boston's Haitian, Irish, and Salvadorian immigrants, many of them undocumented. In the best traditions of social research, she adds dimension to this troubling human concern. Her work gives voice to the fears, the dreams, and the realities of undocumented persons and their families, and to how the 1986 law often served to move them to the margins of society. She shows how this marginalization, in turn, has affected the capacity of public and private human services providers to respond to their needs.

Very important, Hayes traces the failure of IRCA to adequately address the undocumented problem to the nation's ambivalent attitudes, historical and contemporary, toward immigration. Through a historical analysis of the development of immigration policy, she shows how a nation of immigrants has often structured policies that reflect race, ethnic, religious, and class preferences and prejudices. She shows how the interests of business, especially agribusiness, have often been at odds with labor in this policy arena; how employer demand for immigrant labor has been viewed as being in conflict with the interest of the domestic labor force.

IRCA was passed, Dr. Hayes explains, to turn off the spigot of illegal immigration. The amnesty provision, it was hoped, would convert many of the undocumented into legal residents, eventually with citizenship, rendering deportations and other harsh measures unnecessary. Employer sanctions, it was believed, would create significant disincentives for employers to hire the undocumented and less of a reason for foreign nationals to cross U.S. borders illegally. But, as Hayes shows, the compromises fashioned between competing interests and values during the ten years of legislative incubation undermined these provisions. To satisfy interests concerned with restricting immigration, legislative compromises resulted in a more restrictive amnesty than originally intended—far more so than those implemented by other nations that were using this policy tool. The result: A large group of undocumented workers and their families were relegated to permanent underclass status. Conflicts arose between groups concerned with maintaining employment of American workers and those concerned that employer sanctions would discriminate against Hispanics and other ethnic groups, led to a watering down of the employer sanction provisions and to the creation of a guest workers program. Together, such changes undermined the legislation, assuring that neither policy goal was adequately achieved.

Of particular importance, Dr. Hayes's work identifies the implications of the law for the lives of the undocumented. Employer sanctions worsened the conditions of the undocumented and their families. Their day-to-day decisions were often dictated by their fear of discovery. In spite of the creativity of the immigrant serving community agencies, fewer services are available; even fewer sought. Lacking legal recourse, the undocumented are not well positioned to advocate for their families when housing is poor or labor practices unfair. Even so, some thrive, but others recede to the edges of society. IRCA appears to have had a less deleterious effect on the Irish than either

Haitians or Salvadorans, in part a function of their complexion, but also partially a result of the stronger ethnic bonds of the Irish in Boston.

I am appreciative of the hard work, careful scholarship, and commitment that went into the writing of this book. Seeing this book come to publication is a source of satisfaction to me, especially because of what Dr. Hayes brings to this study. As a child of immigrants, her interest in this topic emerges in part from her experience and heart. As a seasoned social work administrator, she draws on front-line experience delivering services to at-risk children and families and new immigrant populations. As a sister of the Good Shepherd and as the leader of its New York, New Jersey, and Massachusetts Province, she brings her passion for social justice to this work. And as a social scientist, she brings the belief that carefully researched information can make a difference to the lives of those who are dispossessed or otherwise vulnerable. Indeed, she has provided us with a product that can.

Introduction

This book is about a specific public policy, the 1986 Immigration Reform and Control Act, and how it directly affected the lives of particular groups of undocumented Haitian, Irish, and Salvadoran immigrants. The vantage point in terms of the policy process is the implementation phase. In this sense, policy is understood not only in terms of what was enacted by Congress but also, and more importantly for the purpose of this book, by what actually occurred consequent to passage.

The research in this book casts a spotlight not only on immigration legislation but also on the end result of the policy process: its impact on human subjects, in this case, silent, vulnerable, and often furtive undocumented immigrants. It is a tale of the human toll on individuals when public policy goes awry. In immigration matters, as with social policy in general, changes in laws affect millions of immigrants for years to come. If those affected are the undocumented, they are necessarily voiceless to protest.

Immigration status is a significant variable when assessing the needs and concerns of immigrant populations. As one study on the service needs of immigrants explains, "One's immigration status determines eligibility for most basic services and entitlements, and it determines the degree of openness with which individuals can identify themselves and advocate for themselves. The advent of IRCA has significantly altered the status of undocumented immigrants and has consequently become a major factor in their lives" (Seiber 1988, p. 57).

The purpose of this book is not to call into question the right of every sovereign nation to control its border. Nor is it an unwise argument for open borders and unfettered immigration. Rather, the purpose is to examine the impact of a policy decision made at the national level and implemented at the local level, and results thereof for the undocumented. The overarching policy issue is the continued presence of the undocumented population within the margins of American society who, as the research will verify, are in a more desperate and disenfranchised state as a result of the implementation of IRCA.

There are two important facts about undocumented immigration into the United States that need to be underscored. One is that undocumented immigration has always existed, and second, that it should be prevented. It has always existed, because, as Laurence Fuchs points out in his book *American Kaleidoscope*, "The most fundamental law of economics [is] at work: supply and demand" (1990, p. 248). When a cheap, mobile, silent, rightless labor force can heighten business profits, depress wages, and keep prices lower for consumers, it can seem like an irresistible cornucopia for everyone—except of course, the undocumented and perhaps low skilled, less educated, secondary market U.S. workers.

From the perspective of the undocumented, individuals and families have crossed international borders for aeons fleeing political repression, war, economic hardship, and abject poverty. Unless and until these root causes are altered, the pattern of migration of peoples into this new millennium will continue unabated.

Undocumented immigration should be prevented because individuals who have entered this country clandestinely have in effect no civil rights, are politically powerless, are easy ploys for exploitation and scapegoating, and have become a desperate underclass that fears apprehension and deportation. They cannot receive social benefits, cannot legally work, and can be arrested, incarcerated, and deported at any time (Bacon 1999, p. 157). Their lives, as the original research in this book will demonstrate, have been reduced to furtive exercises in survival at a very basic primal level.

When the Select Commission on Immigration Reform (SCIRP) issued its final report to Congress, its argument for not allowing an underclass of undocumented immigrants to remain in the United States in a subservient status rested on a single, compelling idea; that the most pernicious effect of undocumented immigration is that "illegality breeds illegality." The commission noted that

This illegal flow, encouraged by employers who provide jobs, has created an underclass of workers who fear apprehension and deportation. Undocumented/illegal migrants, at the mercy of unscrupulous employers and "coyotes" who smuggle them across the border, cannot or will not avail themselves of the protection of U.S. laws. Not only do they suffer, but so does U.S. society. The presence of a substantial number of undocumented/illegal aliens in the U.S. has resulted not only in a disregard for Immigration Law, but in the breaking of minimum wage and occupational safety laws, and statutes against smuggling as well. As long as undocumented migration flouts U.S. Immigration Law, its most devastating impact may be the disregard it breeds for other U.S. laws. (Hesburgh, Final Report 1981, pp. 41, 42)

The argument put forth in this book, therefore, is that the presence of a large undocumented population is deleterious to both the undocumented themselves and the larger society. However, solutions to the social phenomenon of undocumented immigration are extremely complex. Chapter 6 will deal with some of these intricacies. Part of the difficulty with IRCA was its attempt to control our border by turning off the job magnet or the "pull" factor that draws the undocumented to this country; however, insufficient attention had been paid to the "push" factors in terms of the multiplicity of motivations for migration emanating from the home countries of the undocumented. Deteriorating economic, political, and social conditions in developing countries are and will remain the spur for migration to the United States and other developed countries despite measures such as denying illegals basic human services, erecting fences, militarizing our borders, developing tamper-proof ID cards, or denying the undocumented the right to legitimate work or judicial review.

This book tells the story of IRCA, what led up to it, what went wrong with it, and, most importantly, what lessons can be learned from it. It traces the history of undocumented immigration, congressional debate on IRCA, and the implementation of the reform package. It provides direct access to the "faces" of the undocumented in the aftermath of IRCA through an analysis of original research findings on the social and economic impact of IRCA upon the lives of specific groups of undocumented immigrants. Generally speaking, researchers and policy analysts in immigration matters have tended to direct their assessments toward the impact of undocumented immigrants on wages, the labor force, costs to public social services, and changes in American culture. This book reverses this historic trend by looking instead at how a particular piece of immigration legislation has affected the lives of specific groups of undocumented immigrants still living silently in our midst.

The quantitative research profiled Haitian, Irish, and Salvadoran undocumented immigrants and examined their need for and use of social services, comparing their responses with their legalized counterparts. Because the study examined racial and ethnic minority immigrants, it also shed light on the differential impact of IRCA on these specific groups as well. A second research design gleaned qualitative responses from service providers who work directly with the undocumented, which further illuminated the world of the undocumented and provided insights into their actual adaptations in the wake of full implementation of IRCA.

The general theme is America's ambivalence toward its historic lifeline: new immigrants, whether legal or undocumented. This ambivalence is understandable given the enormous complexity that surrounds U.S. immigration policy. It encompasses two key expressions of the nation's sovereignty: the ability to control its borders and the ability to define who the American community is and will be (Moore 1985, p. 613). But as former INS Commissioner Doris Meissner notes, it also evokes strong reactions "in such fundamental areas as race, ethnicity, language, population size, resource depletion, and political culture" (Meissner and Papademetriou 1988, p. 1). The stakes are high in immigration policy because of its potency to affect the labor market, the broader economy, "legal process, human rights, cultural identity, inter-group conflict, foreign policy," and international relations (Moore 1985, p. 613). Although legal immigration is deeply intertwined with undocumented immigration, the focus here is clearly on the latter and the unique kinds of ambivalence that it engenders.

Every so often a piece of legislation is advanced to address a social problem when there is no clarity on what is exactly the social problem to be solved. Undocumented immigration is one such problem. In successive chapters this book pinpoints key policy issues surrounding immigration legislation and teases out the many strands of ambivalence that are embedded in these policy relevant areas. Chapter 2 peels back several layers of ambivalence toward new immigrants that have historically dogged United States legal immigration policy since its inception; namely, issues of race and ethnicity and the conflicting interests of capital and labor. It also analyzes why undocumented immigration reached such a crescendo in the 1970s and 1980s that the stage was set for passage of IRCA. Chapter 3 traces the historical purposes that undocumented immigration has served, in terms of finding temporary workers, and analyzes prior and current research on the impact of undocumented immigration on wages, job displacement, and costs to public social services. In Chapter 4 the legislative history of the main provisions of IRCA, employer sanctions, and the legalization program are unraveled through nearly ten years of honing compromises through interest group politics. In this legislative process the reader bears witness to an immigration policy gradually turning against itself in relation to its proposed goal. Two strategies intended to work in consort with each other ended by being at war with one another, thus producing the effect that is the subject of this inquiry. Chapter 5 uses the results of empirical data gathered during the spring of 1992, derived directly from undocumented immigrants living fully under the implementation of IRCA, and compares their experiences with immigrants who had been accepted for legalization. It examines their social and economic needs and the differential impact of IRCA on racial and ethnic minority undocumented immigrants. It analyzes the research findings on utilization of social services by the undocumented in comparison with legalized immigrants who form a control group; that is, a group similar to the undocumented group on every variable except immigration status. Qualitative data gleaned from interviews with a sample of providers of services to the undocumented is then presented to flesh out the experiences of the undocumented as a result of the implementation of IRCA. The use of social services by the undocumented has long been a potent political bone of contention. Beyond presenting patterns of utilization, the findings from this research hone in on why the undocumented do or do not use social services.

Chapter 6 sums up what can be learned from passage of IRCA from a legislative, policy, and implementation perspective and exposes some of the fault lines that inevitably surface when debate turns to issues surrounding undocumented migration into the United States, such as (1) current legislative initiatives, (2) the deteriorating environment for the undocumented, and (3) the human and civil rights dilemma. Last, some of the challenges and dangers to the nation and the world that await us in this new millennium will be unearthed in their multitudinous complexity. Ultimately, argument in immigration matters turns on what kind of nation we wish to become and what values in our national character we wish to preserve and reflect (Hull 1983, p. 239). Increasingly, the disturbing thought hangs in the mind that as the external threats inherent to the Cold War have dissipated, we have begun to conjure up internal scapegoats, easy targets such as the poor, welfare recipients, and, of course, immigrants, whether legal or undocumented, as foils in this time of global economic insecurity (even in the midst of boom times for some).

I am grateful to the immigrant-serving community who welcomed me into their agencies and shared with me their experiences of working with the undocumented. I am particularly thankful to those individuals who facilitated my access to the undocumented immigrants in the research. Most especially I owe a deep debt of gratitude to the undocumented and legalized immigrants for their gracious trust in participating in the research that undergirds this book. I am deeply indebted to my religious community, the Sisters of the Good Shepherd, for their steadfast support and for nurturing in me an abiding belief in the worth and dignity of every human person.

Chapter 1

Closing the Back Door

> Certainly the growth of a subclass of illegal aliens cannot be in the nation's long-term interest. Once before the nation tried to live with a subclass in its midst. Then the institution was slavery, and the nation is still trying to overcome the legacy of that episode.
>
> V. Briggs

Periodically the nation is moved to heated and often acrimonious debate about the seemingly intractable problem of undocumented immigration into the United States. Witness for example passage of Proposition 187 in California that barred illegal immigrants and their children from public education, nonemergency health care, and social services. This proposition, which the federal court has since found largely unconstitutional, required educators and medical staff to deny public services to those "suspected" of being undocumented and to report them to federal and state authorities. This legislation, which lost an appeal in July 1999, was originally passed into law by 60 percent of Californian voters (Nieves 1999, pp. 1, A15).

Perhaps as an antidote to several states threatening to take the federal government to the Supreme Court to recoup state expenditures on the undocumented, the 1996 federal immigration legislation grants states the option of banning undocumented immigrants from income-based federal nutrition programs such as food stamps and health care services. Absent from the final enactment in the interest of passage was the far more onerous provision of denying public education to the children of the undocumented even if they were native-born Americans. Left unexamined is the long-term impact of these strategies on the future well-being of the nation. Presidential hopeful Patrick Buchanan in his 1996 campaign endorsed the merits of building a "Berlin Wall" along the southern border of the United States and the use of the National Guard as patrol units to keep the fence impermeable. Other proposed solutions include one from a California State University physicist who suggested shaking fluorescent glow dust at the border which would literally tag for capture undocumented immigrants through the use of ultraviolet lights and lasers by border guards. As one immigrant-rights advocate noted regarding this idea, "It's incredible, it's like something out of the twilight zone. The symbolism here is that these are not humans, that these are insects to be sprayed" ("Glowing Dust Urged for Use at U.S. Borders" 1994). In May 1996, ABC news anchor, Peter Jennings, perhaps in an attempt to interject a sense of proportion into a news segment on undocumented immigrants, quipped, "Illegal aliens in America have always been a problem, just ask any Native American."

On a more anecdotal level, allegations of hiring undocumented immigrants, dubbed "Nannygate," scuttled two of President Clinton's Supreme Court nominees, Zoë Baird and Kimba Wood, and President George W. Bush's Labor Secretary Linda Chavez. Running for the U.S. Senate, Michael Huffington of California, after spending a breathtaking $28.3 million of his personal fortune, fell afoul as well. The culprit was (his wife at the time) conservative think tank spokesperson Arianna Huffington, whose hiring of an undocumented person was immediately spotlighted by a voracious media. While this gaffe did not by itself sink Huffington's candidacy, it is indicative of the hot button political issue that undocumented immigration has become. It is at one and the same time a problem that is largely invisible but pervasive. Even the debacle over the American retail giant Walmart and its Kathie Lee Gifford clothing line being subcontracted to Third World sweat factories also uncovered the continued use of undocumented immigrants in sweatshops in the United States. Thought to be a diminishing turn of the nineteenth-century phenomenon in the United States, sweatshops have returned to the limelight with a vengeance. Former Secretary of Labor Robert Reich indicated that there are twenty-two thousand cutting and sewing shops in the United States. More than half of these pay substantially less than minimum wage ("Sweatshops Are Returning to America" 1996). Such conditions act as magnets for undocumented workers.

Historical evidence strongly suggests that groundswell reactions to undocumented immigrants is not a random phenomenon but is instead cyclical. Whenever the economy is in a downspin, questions invariably arise about the negative impact of undocumented immigrants on the economy, the job market, and costs to public social services.

Despite a booming economy in the late 1990s, and through at least the early months of the year 2000, the "bull market" has not proved itself to be the "tide that lifts all boats." Figures published by the congressional budget office indicate that "the wealthiest 2.7 million have as much to spend as the poorest 100 million." While one-fifth of households with the highest income had an increase of 38.2 percent, it should be noted that the income of the lowest one-fifth of households had a 12.7 percent drop in income, while the 1 percent of households with the highest income increased a staggering 119.7 percent (Johnston 1999, p. 14). See Table 1.1 for additional data.

Friedman, in his penetrating work on globalization of the economy, *The Lexus and the Olive Tree*, speaks of the "defining anxiety" of our time as "fear of rapid change from an enemy you can't see, touch or feel—a sense that your job, community or workplace can be changed at any moment by anonymous economic and technological forces that are anything but stable" (1999, p. 11). This kind of uncontrollable economic environment can be the catalyst for future scapegoating of the most unknown among us: the undocumented. Thus, the perennial issue of undocumented immigration and its economic impact on U.S. workers and taxpayers can be seen to persist even in

Table 1.1
A Growing Income Disparity

Household Groups	Share of All Incomes (%)		Average After-Tax Income (Estimated)		Change (%)
	1997	1999	1977	1999	
One-fifth with lowest income	5.7	4.2	$10,000	$8,000	-12.0
Next lowest one-fifth	11.5	9.7	22,100	20,000	-9.5
Middle one-fifth	16.4	14.7	32,400	31,400	-3.1
Next highest one-fifth	22.8	21.3	42,600	45,100	+5.9
One-fifth with highest income	44.2	50.4	74,000	102,300	+38.2
1 Percent with highest income	7.3	12.0	234,700	515,600	+119.7

Source: Congressional Budget Office data analyzed by Center on Budget and Policy Priorities. In *New York Times*, September 5, 1999, p. 14.

Note: Figures do not add to 100 due to rounding.

"bullish times." This is particularly true in border states such as California and Texas, where the impact on the local economy is believed to be more intense. The more latent issue of concern over the ethnic and racial mix in America usually lies silently simmering just beneath the surface. Peter Brimelow's 1995 book, ominously entitled *Alien Nation*, strongly suggests that current immigration policy is leading us head on into a disastrous racial and ethnic national transformation.

The 1986 Immigration Reform and Control Act was enacted more than a decade and a half ago to respond to just such concerns by closing the back door that allowed the undocumented to enter the country with seeming impunity. Ten years in the making, the two key provisions of this reform legislation were intended to stop the illegal flow of undocumented immigrants by turning off the job magnet through imposing sanctions in the form of fines or imprisonment on those who hire the undocumented, and an amnesty program to wipe the slate clean of undocumented immigrants already living in the country. These two provisions were seen as prerequisites to good immigration law enforcement in the future and as a means of eliminating a voiceless, rightless permanent underclass.

Obviously the goal of this legislation, the first U.S. immigration law specifically targeted toward the undocumented, failed in its intended purpose. Had it succeeded, this book need not have been written and the present anti-illegal alien animus might not have reached its current level of stridency. Fifteen years ago, IRCA was referred to by legislators as a generous and compassionate bill that would legalize much of the undocumented population in our midst and then effectively slam the door shut on future undocumented immigration into the United States. It resulted instead in placing a highly vulnerable, silent subclass in deeper jeopardy as a result of public policy. That the legislation failed to close the back door successfully on undocumented immigrants is clear from figures published by the INS in 1997 indicating that "illegal immigration rose to 5 million in 1996" (Schmitt 1997, p. 9).

The following lists the top countries of origin and the estimated number of undocumented residents in the United States as of October 1996:

Mexico	2,700,000	54.1 percent
El Salvador	335,000	6.7 percent
Guatemala	165,000	3.3 percent
Canada	120,000	2.4 percent
Haiti	105,000	2.1 percent
Philippines	95,000	1.9 percent
Honduras	90,000	1.7 percent
Bahamas	70,000	1.4 percent
Nicaragua	70,000	1.4 percent
Poland	70,000	1.4 percent

And, the states with the largest estimated number of undocumented residents in October 1996 follows (Schmitt 1997, p. 9):

California	2,000,000	40.0 percent
Texas	700,000	14.1 percent
New York	540,000	10.8 percent
Florida	350,000	7.0 percent
Illinois	290,000	5.8 percent
New Jersey	135,000	2.7 percent
Arizona	115,000	2.3 percent
Massachusetts	85,000	1.7 percent
Virginia	55,000	1.1 percent
Washington	52,000	1.0 percent

Commenting on these figures, demographer Jeffrey S. Passel from the Urban Institute noted that "the important thing about the INS statistics is, there hasn't been very much of a decline in illegal immigration, if any in recent years" (in Schmitt 1997, p. 9).

It is the hidden story of the undocumented that this book uncovers. Despite what may have been a laudable impulse, in the words of Alan Simpson, coauthor of IRCA, "The intent was to remove a fearful, easily exploitable subclass from our society," the implementation of the legalization and employer sanctions provisions of IRCA have resulted instead in placing in deeper jeopardy the permanent underclass that proponents claimed it would eliminate. (Meissner and Papademetriou 1988, p. 3). Not only does the shadow population continue its subterranean existence within the nation, but it finds itself in a much more vulnerable and dispossessed state than prior to the enactment of IRCA. When the legalization or amnesty program ended on May 5, 1988, a significant number of undocumented immigrants had not benefited from this amnesty provision. Nationwide, 1,551,676 undocumented immigrants had been ultimately accepted for legalization under the Legalizing of Authorized Workers program's provision out of an INS (Immigration and Naturalization Service) estimated figure of 3.9 million eligible undocumented persons (LeMay 1994, p. 83).[1] Five studies on the legalization provision of IRCA have concluded that specific barriers in the legislation prevented the majority of undocumented persons from applying (Heilberger 1987; Meissner 1988; Papademetriou, Meissner, and North 1986; North and Portes 1988; LeMay 1994). The greatest barrier was the eligibility cutoff date of nearly five years which has had the effect of excluding hundreds of thousands of aliens from applying. The "cutoff" date refers to the period of time the undocumented person had to prove that he or she had been living in the United States as an undocumented person. The undocumented immigrant would have to prove through various documents (e.g., rent slips or paycheck stubs) that he or she had resided in the United States "continuously" over the entire eligibility period. Absences of forty-five days or less over this period of time would not make one ineligible. In the case of IRCA, the cutoff date was January 1, 1982, a period of nearly five years. Undocumented immigrants who came after this date were not eligible for legalization. Twelve other countries have implemented legalization programs. Of the twelve countries, eleven countries had a one-year cutoff date, and only one country had a two-year cutoff point (Meissner, Papademetriou, and North 1986, p. 3). A second barrier was the family unity issue. Undocumented aliens had to be individually eligible for legalization. The law was silent on the question of what would happen to relatives of eligible undocumented aliens who were themselves ineligible. Fear of discovery or deportation of these relatives has resulted in many eligible aliens self-selecting out of the amnesty program. Other barriers were the extensive documentation requirements for a population that has survived through dint of avoiding the creation of a paper trail; the application fee of $185 and attendant costs; and the lack of a broad-based public education campaign regarding the legalization program specifically targeted to the undocumented population.

The problem created by the legalization and employer sanctions provisions of IRCA is that for those undocumented aliens who have not been legalized and who subsequently become unemployed or "locked into" their present employment, there is no access to legal employment, and there is no "safety net" of federally funded services and benefits for undocumented aliens and their families. The IRCA legislative package stipulated that the social service delivery system now required proof of residency or legal status as a prerequisite for obtaining social services from federally funded programs. Therefore, it was left up to cities, states, and the private sector to choose to find ways to try to cushion the social and economic impact of this immigration law on individuals and families who were becoming ever more imbedded in a subterranean underclass living in the margins of their communities. The impact of IRCA that has been described here has been largely left unexamined and unaltered. Since it is clear that undocumented immigrants are continuing to make their way to the United States at pre-IRCA levels, it can be anticipated that the residual effect of this reform legislation will have social and economic reverberations within the undocumented population, the human service community, and the larger society in the form of increased levels of poverty, homelessness, substance abuse, domestic violence, and physical and mental health problems. Several authors place the number of undocumented aliens in the United States higher than INS projections. In 1981 the Select Commission on Immigration and Refugee Policy considered the guiding intelligence for immigration reform, placed the number between 3.6 million and 6.0 million; Lasko placed it at 8.2 million; Corwin at 8.6 to 11.3 million; and Thornton at 6.0 to 20.0 million (Gelfand and Bialik-Gilad 1989, p. 23). When it comes to the undocumented, estimates will always remain just that:

estimates. Undocumented immigrants take great pains to remain invisible. The singular logic that they follow is, "If they can be counted, they can be deported." Thus they bend their wills to avoid paper trails at all costs (Crewdson 1983, p. 75).

The problem created by the legalization and employer sanctions provisions of IRCA is that for undocumented immigrants who were not legalized and subsequently became unemployed or locked into their present employment, there is no access to legal employment. Under IRCA the undocumented who were not accepted for legalization were then deprived of the right to work and therefore were deprived of the means to sustenance. In addition, they could be subjected to exploitation by unscrupulous employers since they have no legal recourse, do not have full protection under the law, and under IRCA's stipulation, all federally funded social services require proof of legal status as a prerequisite for obtaining services. One assumption underlying this legislation may have been that employer sanctions would dry up employment opportunities for the undocumented population, thus inducing them to self-deport back to their countries of origin. If the intent of IRCA was to literally starve the undocumented out of the country by cutting off their means of livelihood, there is no evidence to suggest that they are doing so. This exists, despite the fact that under IRCA, the lives of the undocumented began to take on the character of desperate and furtive exercises in survival. The often complex and multilayered reasons why aliens flee their home countries cannot be eradicated by the stroke of the pen that enacted this legislation (Gordon 1988, p. 2). There is however ample evidence that by 1996 the social problem of undocumented immigration had reached a level that once again required federal legislative intervention, indicative of the fact that the policy intervention in 1986 had gone seriously awry. When Congress signed into law the new and more punitive 1996 Illegal Immigration Reform and Immigrant Responsibility Act (IIRIRA), it set in motion a number of legal challenges, among them the denial of due process. In Congress's zeal to expedite quick removal of the undocumented, it eliminated "judicial review" for asylum seekers (Bach 1999, p. 7).

An August 23, 1995 *New York Times* front-page article featured the redoubtable republican mayor of New York City, Rudolph Giuliani, decrying a "U.S. Crackdown on Illegal Aliens." He charged that proposed restrictions "violated basic decency and could throw as many as 60,000 immigration children out of the city's schools and into the streets." Flying in the face of his own conservative right-wing party, Giuliani charged that pending immigration legislation by itself and coupled with the welfare reform legislation was playing "to the public's worst fears of foreigners." The specific proposals that roused his ire "would require public hospitals to report illegal aliens who seek medical treatment and would require public schools to turn away students who are in the country illegally." The feisty mayor noted that these and other proposals "would be both morally and fiscally devastating to cities." In New York City's public schools there are between forty and sixty thousand children whose parents are undocumented. With the threat of being reported and deported, these parents might well decide not to send their children to school. Most likely, their fate would then be left to the mean streets of the city. Likewise, with such a threat hanging over the undocumented in terms of public hospitals, the result might well be avoidance of medical care and thus the proliferation of disease (Firestone 1995, pp. 1, 1A).

The 1996 welfare reform act entitled the Personal Responsibility and Work Opportunity Reconciliation Act imposed new limits on legal immigrants by eliminating access to SSI and food stamps (Espenshade, Baraka, and Huber 1998, p. 28). Mayor Giuliani quickly joined civil rights groups in legally challenging this law, "charging that it violates the constitutional rights of legal immigrants who will lose federal disability and food stamp benefits because they are not citizens." Governors, mayors, state legislators, and civil and immigration rights groups joined efforts by President Clinton to soften the effects of this new legislation on "legal immigrants who were in the country when the law was passed and particularly the elderly and infirm" (Havemann 1999, p. A3). Efforts also focused on restoring benefits to disabled children. Giuliani spoke to this issue at a local news conference in terms of basic equity.

Legal residents pay taxes and contribute on an equal basis with everyone else and now unfortunately the federal government is saying that although they're willing to take their money on an equal basis, when they have difficulty, the federal government is walking away from them. (Havemann 1999, p. A3)

On another level, of course, this clash between Mayor Giuliani and the federal government had far more to do with federal versus state financial responsibility for legal and undocumented immigrants. In June 1998, Clinton restored food stamps eligibility to 75,000 children and 250,000 legal immigrants who had been removed from the rolls by the new law but access to SSI remained unavailable to legal immigrants (Espenshade, Baraka, and Huber 1999, p. 29).

The next chapter tells the story of a nation at war with itself about its historic lifeline, its new immigrants. It is a necessary narrative if we are to understand the genesis of the 1986 immigration law and the outcomes described in the first chapter.

NOTE

1. This study deals with the Legalizing of Authorized Workers program (LAWs), not the Seasonal Agricultural Workers program (SAWs) or the Cuban–Haitian Adjustment program. Under the SAWs program, 1,037,349 foreign agricultural workers were approved for permanent residence status.

Chapter 2

America's Exclusionary Impulse

Our progress in degeneracy appears to me to be pretty rapid. As a nation, we began by directing that "all men are created equal except Negroes." When the Know-Nothings get control, it will read "all men are created equal, except Negroes, and foreigners, and Catholics." When it comes to this I should prefer emigrating to Russia, for instance, when despotism can be taken pure, and without the base alloy of hypocrisy.

Abraham Lincoln

More than any other dynamic, the story of immigration policy in the United States is a tale of ambivalence toward new arrivals. This chapter is organized around a historical analysis that peels back several layers of ambivalence toward new immigrants that has afflicted immigration policy since the nation's inception. This ambivalence toward new arrivals can be seen first of all in America's "exclusionary impulse" toward nonwhite immigrants throughout most of its history and second through the competing and conflicting claims of capital and labor market interests. Third, there is the paradox embodied in undocumented immigration whereby it is denounced on the one hand as a calamity and on the other hand has been permitted to continue. Historian Vernon Briggs points out this irony: "For almost as long as the United States has sought to enforce general restrictions on immigration, there have been parallel legal steps to make formal exceptions for the admission of temporary foreign workers" (1987, p. 995). Over time the creation of these pathways for temporary farm workers paved the way for undocumented immigrants to enter the country even in the midst of overall restrictive immigration policy. This was particularly the case with government-sponsored, successive *bracero* programs that allowed large numbers of undocumented Mexican workers to enter the United States with impunity in order to become "a strong supply of vulnerable Mexican workers who would accept depressed wages and labor standards thereby keeping employer costs down and preventing formation of any effective labor organization" (Fuchs 1990, p. 118). The beneficiaries of undocumented workers in terms of the profit margin have always been employers and American citizens who benefit from cheap labor by paying less at the cash register.

ISSUES OF ETHNICITY AND RACE:
A FIRST LAYER OF AMBIVALENCE

A central premise in this book is that the legalization and employer sanctions provisions of the 1986 law uniquely embodied within the same piece of legislation contradictory and ambivalent attitudes toward immigration which became the seeds of its implementation difficulties. In this chapter, beyond a broad-stroked descriptive outline of America's checkered history in terms of its treatment of newcomers, the various strands of ethnicity and race and acquisitive capitalism's classic tug of war with the demands of labor will be shown to contribute substantially to a dualistic attitude toward immigrants, whether legal or undocumented, which finally spawned legislation in 1986 that was so profoundly compromised that it could not be implemented with any rational hope of success. Its ineffectiveness can be seen most clearly in the need to pass mean-spirited and regressive immigration legislation in 1996 with draconian results for legal immigrants as well as their undocumented counterparts. When combined with the 1996 welfare reform legislation, which eliminated a vast array of federal benefits to legal immigrants, the cumulative effect can be said to be devastating. Legal immigrants who have paid taxes for years and have built up considerable equity in the United States are no longer eligible for most public benefits no matter how young or old or sick or disabled they are.

At first glance, America's initial welcome mat to new arrivals is impressive. Over a two-hundred-year period, forty-nine million persons came to the United States from as many as 155 different countries as of 1980 Census figures (LeMay 1987, p. xi). Despite these positive statistics, it is also true to say that Americans have always been of two minds about immigration. On the one hand, since most Americans are either immigrants themselves or descendants of immigrants (except of course, Native Americans), the idea of a nation of nations is central to the national psyche. On the other hand, "the ancient human suspicion of strangers has produced immigration laws" that have been restrictive, discriminatory, and racist, suggestive of a deep, long-standing ambivalence toward newcomers ("Doors and Walls" 1987, p. 294). In immigration matters, America began on an idealistic note. Our first President George Washington himself set the tone:

The bosom of America is open to receive not only the opulent and respectable stranger, but the oppressed and persecuted of all Nations and Religions; whom we shall welcome to a participation of all our rights and privileges, if by decency and propriety of conduct they appear to merit the enjoyment. (In LeMay 1987, pp. 7, 9)

However, the reality was that 80 percent of American society during this initial time period was of British stock, with the rest of the Caucasian population coming from German or Dutch roots. Historian Elizabeth Midgley points out that by 1830, 95 percent of white Americans could be described as "highly fertile English-speaking Protestants, Americans of several generations' standing . . . involuntary migrants [from Africa] were disregarded as an element in the national culture" (1983, p. 41). Also, during this period new immigration accounted for only 6 percent of American's population growth. The potato famines in Ireland and the economic depressions in Germany in the 1830s and 1840s broke through this "ethnic deadlock" and set in motion intense negative reactions to foreigners that culminated in the formation of nativist movements such as the Know Nothing political party. Seeking to block admission of Catholics in the northeast and Chinese immigrants in the west, anti-Irish, anti-Catholic sentiments were most vividly captured by inventor Samuel F. B. Morse in his vitriolic warning:

How is it possible that foreign turbulence imported by shiploads, that riot and ignorance in hundreds of thousands of human priest-controlled machines should suddenly be thrown into our society and not produce turbulence and excess? Could one throw mud into pure water and not disturb its clearness? (Fuchs, Forbes, in Hesburgh, Staff Report 1981, p. 171).

Such nativistic rantings did not, however, influence an immigration policy that responded instead to the burgeoning economic need in the 1840s for cheap foreign labor in cities, factories, coalmines, mills, the first transcontinental railroad, and the taming of the west. All these projects "created a virtually insatiable need for immigrants" (LeMay 1987, p. 10).

Between 1890 and 1914, fifteen million immigrants entered the United States. This represented about one-third of the population growth during this period. However, it was not the sheer numbers of newcomers but rather the change in their national origins that sounded the alarm bell. In a nutshell, in 1882, 87 percent of the new arrivals came from Northern and Western Europe. By 1907, "the proportions were reversed" with 81 percent coming from Southern and Eastern Europe and 19 percent coming from Northern and Western Europe (Midgley 1983, p. 42).

With pen in hand writing his *History of the American People*, Woodrow Wilson made clear his disdain for the new arrivals:

Immigrants poured steadily in as before, but with alterations which students of affairs marked with uneasiness. . . . Now there came multitudes of men of lowest class from the south of Italy and some of the meanest sort out of Hungary and Poland, men out of the ranks where there was neither skill nor energy nor any initiative of quick intelligence; and they came in numbers which increased from year to year, as if the countries of the south of Europe were disburdening themselves of the more sordid and hapless elements of their population. (Midgley 1983, p. 42)

By 1882 fear of declining job opportunities for Americans combined with racial and ethnic prejudice to foster passage of the Chinese Exclusion Act of 1882, which prohibited Chinese from becoming U.S. citizens, and suspended further immigration for a ten-year period. This act was extended in 1897, 1902, and 1904. What needs to be made clear is that beyond laws to exclude Chinese, overall immigration continued at the rate of 1.2 million in 1907 and approximately a million a year up until 1910 (Morris 1985, p. 14).

Midgley pinpoints the 1890s as the period of time that "ineradicable foreignness became the issue, that racism came to play a decisive role in attitudes towards immigration." She adds that it was then that "cultural differences between the 'old' immigration and the 'new' were transformed in the minds of many into immutable hereditary distinctions" (1983, pp. 43, 44). Historians, sociologists, and biologists began to publish a rash of pseudoscientific studies "purporting to document the racial inferiority of non–Anglo-Saxons and the potential dangers to American society." In his "Tide of Economic Thought," Census Superintendent Francis A. Walker wrote in 1890 that the new immigrants were drawn from "great stagnant pools of population which no current of intellectual or moral activity had stirred for ages" (Morris 1985, p. 18).

When Congress set up the Dillingham Commission in 1907 to study immigration policy, the findings once again stressed racial and cultural factors. Its authors, Midgley notes, "sharpened, sanctioned and reinforced the already widespread, popular distinction between the 'new' and the 'old' immigration" (1983, p. 46). Rather than examining the more universal human traits to be found in various immigration streams, their focus zeroed in on traits purported to be particular to certain nations:

The new immigration as a class is far less intelligent than the old. . . . Generally speaking, they are actuated in coming by different ideals, for the old immigration came to be part of the country while the new, in large measure, comes with the intention of profiting in a pecuniary way, by the superior advantages of the new world and then returning to the old country. (Midgley 1983, p. 46)

The commission added proverbial fuel to the fire by further noting that immigration "had widespread adverse effects on the country and that immigrants tended to cluster in overcrowded urban ghettos, and to be overrepresented in mental hospitals" (Morris 1985, p. 19). These findings confirmed the pseudoscientific assertions that immigrants from Southern and Eastern Europe were racially and ethnically inferior.

Congress's favorable response to the Dillingham report can be seen in the introduction of literacy requirements for immigrants in 1917 and in the quota laws adopted in 1921. A report to the House Committee on Immigration and Naturalization in 1922 reinforced the notion that the impact of racial and ethnic diversity in the immigration pool was cause for alarm. Eugenicist Harry H. Laughlin's report stressed that scientific evidence showed "all foreigners were inferior" particularly "those from Southern and Eastern Europe." His conclusion was that "the surest biological principle to direct the future of America along safe and sound racial channels is to control the hereditary quality of the immigration stream" (Morris 1985, p. 19).

In 1924 Congress passed the National Origins Act, which it amended in 1928. Through this legislation a ceiling of 150,000 immigrants per year was established as well as a quota for each nationality equal to 2 percent of that nationality living in the United States *according to the 1890 census*. Clearly, such a quota system favored the countries of Western and Northern Europe because they had already provided many more immigrants to the United States by 1890 "than the nations of Eastern and Southern Europe, Asia, Africa, and Latin America" (Carrasco 1987, p. 3, emphasis added).

That the intent of the 1924 quota law was to confine immigration as much as possible to Western and Northern European immigrants was made blatantly clear by the minority report, which reads:

The obvious purpose of this discrimination is the adoption of an unfounded anthropological theory that the nations which are favored are the progeny of fictitious and hitherto unsuspected Nordic ancestors, while those discriminated against are not classified as belonging to that mythical ancestral stock. No scientific evidence worthy of consideration was introduced to substantiate this pseudo-scientific proposition. It is pure fiction and the creation of a journalistic imagination. (U.S. Commission on Civil Rights 1980, p. 9)

At two specific times, from 1929 to 1934, and 1954 to 1958, discriminatory immigration policies were directed at our southern neighbors; Mexican immigrants. During these two "sweeps," dubbed a "Repatriation Campaign" in the first instance and "Operation Wetback" in the second, the United States moved millions of persons to Mexico, many of whom were American citizens, without benefit of formal deportation proceedings (Carrasco 1987, p. 3).

This pattern of abuse of U.S. citizens occurred again in 1942 when 112,000 Japanese Americans were forcibly removed from their West Coast homes and placed in concentration camps. It is this episode that haunts the pages of Robert Guterson's 1994 bestseller *Snow Falling on Cedars*.

Most tragic of all, Jewish refugee children from Europe fleeing the Nazis at the outbreak of World War II were prevented from entering the United States in 1939. The 1981 Select Commission on Immigration and Refugee Policy reports this dark blot on America's history in these words: "In what may have been the cruelest single action in U.S. Immigration the U.S. Congress in 1939 defeated a bill to rescue 20,000 children from Nazi Germany, despite the willingness of U.S. families to sponsor them, on the grounds that the children would exceed the German quota" (Fuchs, Forbes, in Hesburgh, Staff Report 1981, p. 199).

In 1952, Congress passed immigration legislation that has provided the principles governing immigration up to the mid-1990s, namely (1) reunification of families, (2) protection of the domestic labor force, and (3) immigration of persons with needed skills. Only in 1996 was the first of these three elements, which had guided immigration policy over several decades, tinkered with: the family reunification principle. The Illegal Immigration Reform and Responsibility Act of 1996 profoundly altered the family reunification emphasis by placing burdensome restrictions on immigrants trying to bring even close family members to the United States. The legislation favors the wealthiest members of U.S. society and requires sponsors to sign a legally binding affidavit that they earn at least 125 percent of the poverty level. At the very least, the new act smacks of economic elitism and effectively nullifies family reunification as a guiding value in immigration policy.

Although the 1952 immigration policy known as the McCarren–Walter Act removed barriers to Asian immigration, it retained the highly biased national origins system that gave free reign for immigrants from Western Europe to enter the United States without restrictions. Hubert Humphrey decried the dark shadow of racism that the national origins policy cast upon the United States in describing it as

A racist philosophy. It is a philosophy of fear, suspicion and distrust of the foreigners outside our country, and of aliens within our country. . . . This philosophy is founded on the assumption that America is under the constant threat of losing her Anglo-Saxon character because of immigration and that the so-called bloodstock of America, described as Anglo-Saxon and Nordic, is the basis of America and must be preserved from contamination by foreign immigrants. (Reimers, in Chiswick 1982, p. 26)

Even more starkly, fellow liberal Senator Hubert Lehman honed in on the racist nature of the national origins law. In essence he described "its striking similarity to the basic racial philosophy officially espoused so unfortunately and with such tragic consequences in Nazi Germany a few short years ago" (Reimers, in Chiswick 1982, p. 26).

The impact of racial and ethnic prejudice began to wane in the aftermath of World War II as newly independent nations such as India and the Philippines were allowed immigration quotas for the first time, thus ending the exclusion of their nationals. The wartime alliance between the United States and China led to the repeal of the Chinese Exclusion Law in 1943. However, the national origins principles still excluded Asian and African immigrants (Morris 1985, pp. 20–21).

THE 1965 IMMIGRATION LAW:
AN IDEAL THAT BACKFIRED

Finally in 1965 the national origins system was called into question and defeated. As early as 1952 President Harry Truman spoke against the unfairness of the national origins law to Southern Europeans and Asians in unmistakably clear terms:

The basis of this quota system was false and unworthy in 1924. It is even worse now. At the present time this quota system keeps out the very people we want to bring in. It is incredible to me that, in this year of 1952, we should again be enacting into law such a slur on the patriotism, the capacity, and the decency of a large part of our citizenry. . . . In no other realm of our national life are we so hampered and stultified by the dead hand of the past as we are in this field of immigration. (Briggs 1984, p. 60)

Although Congress did not rescind the national origins policy in response to Truman's admonition, Truman was able to lay the foundation for its demise by creating a presidential commission to study immigration policy. In 1953 the commission report "Whom Shall We Welcome?" published its findings: "The major disruptive influence in our immigration law is the racial and national discrimination caused by the national origins system"; it should be replaced by a "unified quota system which would allocate visas without regard to national origin, race, creed, or color" (Midgley 1985, p. 50).

Increasingly, as the United States assumed a central leadership role on the world front, there was "a growing desire to shed so prominent a symbol of American racism as the National Origins principle" (Morris 1985, p. 21). By the late 1960s, a massive civil rights movement catapulted the nation into a reexamination of its public policies in the light of new insights into racism and discrimination. The Civil Rights Act of 1964 coupled with the Voting Rights Act helped to usher in a new era in immigration policy that sounded the death knoll for the national origins concept. Passage of the 1965 Immigration and Nationality Act purged race and ethnicity from the system as a criteria for entry into the United States. In its place a preference system for the allocation of visas for foreign states was established. The new emphasis was on family reunification rather than the earlier emphasis on labor market considerations (Briggs 1984, p. 65). The 1952 Immigration Act had earmarked 50 percent of exclusively available visas for labor force needs. This group was given priority over other admissions categories up to 1965. The 1965 immigration law established a preference system for the allocation of immigration visas within each foreign state (see Table 2.1).

According to the 1965 preference system, 74 percent of persons seeking entry into the United States had to have a relative residing in the United States. In this new schema, spouses, minors, and parents of U.S. citizens who were over the age of twenty-one were not considered part of the ceiling applied to hemispheres or per country counts. As a result since 1965, immigration of immediate relatives had averaged, on an annual basis, between one-hundred thousand and one-hundred-fifty thousand in excess of the statutory limits (Briggs 1984, p. 64).

However, a residue of prior discrimination against eastern nations continued to operate under the 1965 act in that it set an annual limit of twenty-thousand visas for any single eastern nation. No such limit was set for any Western Hemisphere country. Within the seven-preference system, admissions from Eastern nations were based on a "first-come first-served basis" (Briggs 1984, p. 64). However, forces opposed to the demise of the now discredited national origins system hoped to change the name without actually changing the game in terms of admissions to the United States (1984, p. 69). The idea behind this was that if family reunification were the main criteria, then it would be possible to maintain the same racial and ethnic mix in America as when national origins was the criteria. Citizens from countries such as Asia and Eastern European nations had little opportunity to come to the United States prior to 1965 and therefore would be unable to effectively use the family reunification preference system. A number of Japanese Americans foresaw the implications of this plan for Asian-Pacific rim countries and protested accordingly. They noted that "only one half of one percent" of the U.S. population was of Asian descent, and therefore eliminating "race as a matter of principle, in actual operation immigration will still be controlled by the now discredited national origins system" (Briggs 1984, p. 69). Despite legitimate protests such as this, the provision was adopted without amendment.

A second way in which discrimination and a "lingering nativism" was in evidence in the 1965 law were amendments to the legislation which Congress inserted in a negative response to the influx of dark-skinned Spanish-speaking immigrants from Central and South America and Mexico (Fuchs, Forbes, in Hesburgh, Staff Report 1981, p. 208). As indicated, the previous 1952 immigration law had not placed any limit on immigration from the Western Hemisphere. However, as negative reactions solidified around concern for the social and economic impact of these new arrivals on American society, the legislature hastened to restrict Western Hemisphere immigration "as the price to be paid for abolishing the national origins system" (Fuchs, Forbes, in Hesburgh, Staff Report 1981, p. 208). This provision went into effect on July 1, 1968, placing a ceiling on immigration from the Western Hemisphere at 120,000

Table 2.1
The 1965 Immigration and Nationality Act Preference System

Preference	Category	Maximum Proportion of Total Admitted
First	Unmarried sons and daughters of United States citizens	20%
Second	Spouses and unmarried sons and daughters of aliens lawfully admitted for permanent residence	20 plus any not required by first preference
Third	Members of the professions, scientists, and artists of exceptional talent	10
Fourth	Married sons and daughters of U.S. citizens	20 plus any not required by first preference
Fifth	Brothers and sisters of U.S. citizens	24 plus any not required by first four preferences
Sixth	Skilled and unskilled workers in occupations for which labor is in short supply	10
Seventh	Refugees to whom conditional entry or adjustment may be given	6
Nonpreference	Any applicant	Numbers not used by preceding preferences

Source: V. M. Briggs, *Immigration Policy and the American Labor Force*. Baltimore: Johns Hopkins University Press, 1984, p. 65.

and for the Eastern Hemisphere at 170,000. Proponents of a ceiling, while avoiding blatantly racist terminology, spoke instead of Latin America and Caribbean immigrants as "different" and insisted that America not become the "dumping ground" for "surplus populations" (Reimers 1985, p. 81).

Despite such occasional lapses into discrimination in immigration policy, the 1965 immigration policy was hailed, in conjunction with the civil rights legislation of the 1960s, as "tearing down the institutional racism of previous U.S. immigration legislation" (Papademetriou and Miller 1983, p. 11). In replacing the racially and ethnically biased national origins policy with a more neutral admissions program, the 1965 legislation intentionally changed the character of U.S. immigration by announcing that henceforth "it would look impartially on the world" (Anzovin 1985, p. 9).

However, because of this 1965 legislation, significant changes in the immigration stream occurred that, in time, would hasten in the next decade long immigration debate that would culminate in the passage of the 1986 Immigration Reform and Control Act. In the process, old ghosts of racial and ethnic tensions would be resurrected once again, albeit dressed in more muted and restrained political language.

The increase in the numbers of undocumented immigrants can be accounted for in part by the termination after twenty years of the *bracero* program which allowed Mexican workers to cross over the border to work for U.S. employers on a temporary basis. *Bracero* means literally "one who works with his arms" (Briggs 1984, p. 98). This program, begun first in 1917 and used on a larger scale in 1942, ended almost at the same time as the enactment of the 1965 immigration law (Papademetriou and Miller 1983, p. 10).

For several immigration scholars (Glazer 1985; Briggs 1987; LeMay 1987; Fuchs 1990; and Midgley 1983), undocumented immigration may have been a logical continuation of the pattern of seasonal migration set in motion by the *bracero* program. Very quickly, as Nathan Glazer points out, undocumented immigration became much more than that. Several Latin American countries (e.g., El Salvador and Nicaragua) developed deep political and economic troubles in the 1970s and 1980s resulting in large streams of undocumented Latin Americans crossing the border into the United States (1985, p. 10).

The increase in Western Hemisphere legal immigration can be accounted for by the fact that "prior to 1968, immigration from this region was unrestricted." From 1968 to 1976 the Western Hemisphere was held to a ceiling but preference categories did not apply. In this way "a broad range of individuals from the Western Hemisphere" could enter the United States and, in turn, could use their presence in the country to leverage for the reunification of family members and relatives through the family preference categories (Briggs 1984, p. 79).

This process does not explain how immigration from Southeast Asia increased so rapidly. In 1965 Congress fully expected Asian immigration to be minimal. The answer lies in the way Asians were able to capitalize on the preference system, in particular the refugee provisions of the 1965 system. In the years 1975 to 1981, more than 500,000 refugees were admitted from Vietnam, Cambodia, and Laos. Legal immigrants made their way to the United States from the Philippines, Taiwan, Korea, India, and Hong Kong, often making use of the occupational preference categories such as health care and the fields of science and engineering, in which they were dominant. The provision for professionals in general also proved helpful to Asian immigrants who could then petition for family members through the reunification provision. Once admitted, new arrivals could also gain admission for their relatives as well (Briggs 1984, p. 79).

There was, however, a reverse aspect to these processes for the sending countries. As the Deputy Minister for Education for Taiwan stated, "We have given America the cream of our youth, not our problem people; it improves your work force but it is our brain drain problem" (Briggs 19984, p. 82).

Congress had not foreseen the volume of immigration from Mexico and the Caribbean basin and the resulting backlog in processing applications. Many applicants had to wait for more than three years to be united with their families and therefore, as Papademetriou and Miller point out, the situation may well have "spurred illegal immigration" (1983, p. 15).

In sum, by 1979 thirteen percent of immigration into the United States was from Europe while "eighty-one percent came from Asia and Latin America including Mexico and the Caribbean" (Morris 1985, p. 57). In total, the increase in immigration after passage of the 1965 law over the next ten years was nearly 60 percent (LeMay 1987, p. 114).

In terms of legal immigrants, the 1980 total was 800,000 including 130,000 Haitian and Cuban special "entrants." As legal immigration from Europe declined, Asian immigration rose from 362,000 to 1.5 million; African immigration rose from 33,000 to 87,000; South American immigration from 219,000 to 266,000; and Mexican immigration from 432,000 to 624,000 (Sellers 1984, pp. 155, 156). By 1980, the Census Bureau reported that there were approximately 15 million Hispanics in the United States. Beyond this, figures approximating the numbers of undocumented immigrants were estimated to be in the range of 2.9 million to 5.7 million (Abrams 1984, p. 112).

Immigration scholar Michael LeMay presents Professor Leibowitz's argument that the 1980 change in the definition of "refugee" increased the numbers eligible for asylum "from 3 million to nearly 13 million people" (1987, p. 121). This change entailed a broadening of the category of refugee to include those who have a "well-founded fear of persecution on account of race, religion, nationality, membership in a social group, or political opinion" (Cockcroft 1986, p. 215). The earlier, more restrictive definition simply included those fleeing communism or fleeing the Middle East.

From a political perspective, the 1980 act continued to be used in such a manner that those fleeing communist countries such as Cuba were welcomed, whereas those refugees fleeing violence and right-wing dictatorships in Haiti or El Salvador were turned away. In the case of the U.S.–backed dictatorship in El Salvador, refugees were returned to their country and for some, "to their deaths" (Cockcroft 1986, p. 215).

Collectively, the new waves of immigrants entering the United States in the 1980s were characterized by an unprecedented number of Asians and Hispanics. The nation they were entering was experiencing an energy crisis, an economy in a tailspin, and a grinding unemployment problem. Of equal concern, they were entering a nation with a well-documented history of racial and ethnic discrimination, fresh from its own disastrous and unsuccessful war in southeast Asia (Sellers 1984, p. 156). Simcox, in his 1988 book *Analy-*

sis of U.S. Immigration in the 1980s, pinpoints several trends and events that contributed to a shift in the public mind that culminated in a sense of "compassion fatigue" regarding new immigrants (p. 3).

Among the incidents that reinforced then Attorney General William French Smith's perception in 1981 that "we have lost control of our borders" were

- The friction created by the assimilation and attendant costs of resettlement of over one million refugees, the majority from southwest Asia.
- The apprehension of over one million Mexican undocumented immigrants by 1976. This figure surged by 25 percent in 1983 at a time when U.S. unemployment had reached 10 percent.
- The Mariel boatlift, which created the disturbing feeling that "a fraying American Immigration Policy was being made not in Washington" but cynically in Havana.
- The inability in 1979 of the Immigration and Naturalization Service to "find" fifty-thousand politically disruptive Iranian students on study visas to the United States. The idea at the time was to hold them accountable to the terms of their visas, if indeed they had them.
- The 1981 *Doe v. Plyer* Supreme Court decision that assured undocumented immigrant children free public school education at taxpayers' expense.
- Rising public concern over crime among immigrants and refugees, in particular crime among the Mariel boatlift refugees and drug-related crime in Florida.
- "The spread of bilingualism and multi-lingualism in the 70s," resistance to it, and the public perception that the impact of immigration was too pervasive, too rapid, and indeed, unwelcome (Simcox 1988, pp. 3, 4).

In summary, inexplicably, through a host of events and the intended and unintended effects of the 1965 Immigration Act, the policy that had sought to eliminate discrimination in immigration matter ended up exacerbating the negative reactions it had explicitly aimed at eradicating.

The momentum for passage of the more restrictive 1986 legislation (IRCA) with its specific focus on undocumented immigration began with the implementation of the 1965 Immigration Act. Specifically, the 1965 amendments "eliminated the discriminatory national origins system in favor of the equal number of immigrant visas for each nation." This decision dramatically altered the ethnic and racial origins of the immigrant stream. Through its preference system, the 1965 bill "substantially redirected overall immigration preferences towards spouses, minor children, and parents of United States citizens by allowing them to immigrate with no numerical limitations" (Keely 1989, p. 203). A second development was the admission of large number of political refugees, particularly from Cuba and Indochina. Third, there was an increase in undocumented immigration to the United States, spawned in part by the end of the *bracero* program and the use of specially admitted "temporary" farm workers called H-2 workers. Numerical limits placed on Third World countries such as Mexico and those of the Caribbean and Latin America had the effect of inducing many immigrants to seek illegal entry when other means had failed them. Finally, as Bean, Schmandt, and Weintraub (1989) have pointed out, the increase in the numbers of legal immigrants over the last twenty years had included "higher proportions of Hispanics and Asians," and since most of the undocumented aliens in the United States are of the same "national origins," confusion may have existed in the public mind about which of these two distinct populations (legal or undocumented) were increasing in volume and with what results for the domestic population (1989, p. 106).

Through the 1965 immigration policy decision and its aftermath, and the continued attraction that many U.S. employers felt toward hiring an inexpensive and pliable labor force, the United States has in a sense "created" its own illegal immigration problem—marked as it is by the ambivalence of wanting the undocumented as workers but not wanting them as human persons.

Reflecting on this general climate, Papademetriou and Miller noted that "had it not been for the nexus of Indo-Chinese/Cuban/Haitian refugees, the topic [of immigration] might not have become a centerpiece on the United States political agenda." Prior to this point, immigration was viewed as "relevant primarily to the southwestern regions." As the debate on legal and illegal emigration became more all-encompassing in the 1970s and 1980s, it reverted at times "to shrill warnings" about the "Hispanicization" of the United States. Controversy in the 1970s and early 1980s over undocumented immigrants were couched at times in terms such as "intolerable burdens," "racial and cultural contaminants," "free-loaders," "welfare cheats," and "mañana minded" (1983, p. 26).

Writing in the 1980s, Maxine Sellers pointed out that "overtly racist statements against immigration," so common in the past, were "rarely heard" in immigration debate. However, she pointed out that "economically troubled times have been marked" by a disconcerting trend: "an increase in the activities of such overtly racist fringe groups as the American Nazi Party and the Ku Klux Klan." Somewhat coincidentally, "a new cadre of academicians had published controversial findings stressing the controlling role of heredity in human evolution." In particular, Sellers pointed out that educational psychologist Arthur Jenson had made the claim "that I.Q. tests prove that black children are innately less intelligent than white children." In light of such claims and the recent increase in Asian and Hispanic immigrants that are "altering" the ratio between mainstream whites and minorities, "racism," according to Sellers, "cannot be ruled out as a hidden motive in the current swing towards" restrictionist immigration policy (1984, p. 161). Portes and Kincaid are more direct in their assessment:

The casting of recent immigrants to this country as scapegoats in times of social and economic distress has been a recurrent phenomenon in American History. The late 1970s and early 1980s provided but the latest example. If the arguments were no longer couched in blatantly racist and segregationist terms, immigration populations still offered an easy target for anxieties over high unemployment rates, public spending and taxation, the quality of schools, and so forth. The call to restore the rule of law and restrict immigration thus had widespread popular appeal. (1985, p. 74)

On the other hand, Morris (1985) and Papademetriou and Miller (1983) point to a new element that found expression for the first time in immigration debate; that is, reasoned concerns about basic human rights for undocumented persons in the United States who are living beyond the pale of the law. According to Reimers, concern was expressed by some liberals that "the nation was witnessing the growth of a permanent underclass of people confined to the secondary labor market with little prospect of escape in the future" (1985, p. 229). In 1983, Vernon Briggs expressed his concern in more disquieting imagery:

Certainly the growth of a subclass of illegal aliens cannot be in the nation's long-term interest. Once before the nation tried to live with a subclass in its midst. Then the institution was slavery, and the nation is still trying to overcome the legacy of that episode. It is an experience that should not be repeated. (In Reimers 1985, p. 230)

However, beyond these sentiments, as LeMay notes, it has always been economic need that has prevailed as one of the strongest driving forces behind immigration policy. U.S. immigration policy mirrors reactions to changes in the ethnic and racial composition of the immigrant stream, but it also reflects the country's perceived needs at various times "in response to changing economic conditions" (1985, p. 5, 10).

CONFLICTING CLAIMS OF CAPITAL AND LABOR: A SECOND LAYER OF AMBIVALENCE

While it is axiomatic to refer to America as a "nation of immigrants" and a "nation of nations," even a cursory review of the "track record" of U.S. immigration policy suggests that a profound ambivalence exists; that what lies beneath a rhetoric of welcome are policies that quite often have been discriminatory, racist, and xenophobic. "Ambivalence" is defined by Webster as "a continual fluctuation, as between one thing and its opposite." It is clear that the welcome extended to many immigrants became its opposite for a significant number of other groups over much of the nation's history. Morris notes that "non-whites were virtually excluded for most of the country's history" (1985, p. 12).

From another perspective, however, the nation's ambivalence toward newcomers embodied in U.S. immigration policy "can best be understood within the parameters of capital and labor relations" (Papademetriou and Miller 1983, p. 8). Some labor economists, among them Ehrenberg and Piore, see the overall labor market as divided into two noncompeting sectors: primary and secondary markets. The basic distinction between these two markets is that the primary sector has offered relatively high wages, stable employment, good working conditions, and opportunities for advancement, while the secondary sector tends to have "low wage, unstable and dead-end jobs," and poor working conditions (Ehrenberg and Smith 1982, p. 410). Within this dual labor market theory, mobility between the two sectors is thought to be quite limited. The distinction between these two labor markets is important in examining the impact of legal and undocumented immigration on the labor market. Research findings available in the years prior to the enactment of IRCA yielded the following insights and conclusions.

Julian Simon in his testimony before the Select Commission hearings indicated that "immigrants create jobs as well as take them. They create them by starting new businesses for themselves. They create jobs, either directly or indirectly, when their goods are exported" (in Hesburgh 1981, p. 273). What remains in dispute, despite extensive research, is the question of whether new immigrants displace or compete with unskilled native laborers for secondary sector jobs. "The heated debate is over how many are hurt and how badly," over and against how others may benefit (LeMay 1987, p. 133). Barry Chiswick points out that "immigrants do not have a uniform impact on the native population. Some native groups gain and others lose. The level and distribution of the impact depends on the relative skill characteristics of the immigrants" (in Hesburgh 1981, p. 273).

Other economists perceive the impact of immigration as more complex. They theorize that immigrants affect job opportunities and earnings of different groups of native workers not simply in relation to their level of skills, but also in relation to specific locales. Several empirical studies have examined localized effects of legal immigration on specific groups.

Muller in 1984, and with Espenshade in 1985, compared labor market conditions in Los Angeles County with the rest of the United States in relation to immigration. The question that the researchers raised was "to what extent did the influx of immigrants entering Southern California in the 1970s reduce the jobs available to non-immigrant workers?" Their answer was "little if at all" changed in the availability of jobs as a result of immigration. Hispanics filled a large number of the jobs added during the decade in question, while job opportunities for U.S. workers were not reduced (in Simon 1989, p. 229).

In a second cross-sectional study Muller and Espenshade looked at black employment in 247 metropolitan areas in the United States, and fifty-one metropolitan areas in California, New Mexico, and Arizona, states with large numbers of Mexicans. The researchers "regressed the rate of unemployment among blacks upon the percentage of Hispanics in the population, holding constant the percentage change in the population between 1970 and 1980, the percentage of income from construction and durable goods industries, the percentage of blacks with a high school education, and the rate of unemployment for whites." Their findings were that black unemployment rates were not heightened by an increase "in the proportion of Mexican immigrants in a local labor market." In the main, "variations in black unemployment rates among metropolitan areas can be attributed to differences in black educational attainment, in the rate of population growth, and in the degree of durable goods manufacturing and construction" (in Simon 1989, p. 230). However, the findings with regard to wages are a different story; Muller concludes:

There is little doubt that wages in several occupations and industries rise more slowly in Los Angeles than elsewhere as low-skilled immigrants, primarily Hispanics, entered the labor force . . . most notably in the manufacturing sector. (Simon 1989, p. 230)

Muller notes that this is particularly true in the relatively low-wage industries such as "in apparel and textile productions and in relatively low-wage industries such as restaurants, personal services, and hotels where many Mexicans are employed" (in Simon 1989, p. 230).

Similarly, in a study using Census Bureau and Department of Labor data, McCarthy and Valdez looked at employment, unemployment, wages, and population for Los Angeles and California compared to the United States as a whole. Their findings include the following:

Immigration appears to have provided a net benefit to the California economy by supporting industrial and manufacturing growth. Their negative labor market effects have been minor and concentrated among the native-born Latino population. (In Simon 1989, p. 234)

DeFreitas investigated the effects of Hispanic workers, mostly undocumented, on male and female groups of Anglos, blacks, and Hispanics. He separated the groups into native and foreign born who immigrated between 1975 and 1980. His findings were that there was "no negative effect upon the wages of any group except those of black females":

For all low-skilled native men the results indicate that there are no significant negative effects on their wage levels from recent Hispanic immigration. In fact, such migration has a significantly positive influence on Anglo-male earnings. . . . The only persons whose wages appear to have been somewhat adversely affected by illegal migration since the mid-70s are black women. (In Simon 1989, p. 235)

Low-skilled immigrants, such as many of the immigrants from Mexico or the Caribbean, tend to become part of the secondary market. This tends to deflect any potential adverse effects away from the majority of American workers, who fall into the primary market category. When the impact of undocumented immigration is factored into questions regarding labor market effect, researchers are more sharply divided on the question of job displacement, depression of wages, and working conditions. Research on the specific effects of undocumented immigration on wages and job displacement will be considered in some detail in the next chapter.

Several immigration authors (Briggs 1984; Glazer 1985; LeMay 1987; Papademetriou and Miller 1983; Morris 1985) view capital as having "an almost uninterrupted series of victories" over labor in the history of immigration policy (Papademetriou 1983, p. 8). As Morris suggests, "One of the most powerful forces to affect immigration policy has been the fear that immigrants will displace domestic workers, depress wages, and contribute to poor working conditions" (1985, p. 15). On the other hand, the interests of capital and employers lie in a workforce which Papademetriou and Miller describe as having "little social consciousness, no political power, and an essentially temporary and revocable nature." This kind of labor force "enabled capital to remain profitable in marginal enterprises by postponing" costs associated with competitive wages, benefits, and safe working conditions (1983, p. 9).

Organized labor "was most successful in obtaining restrictive and/or exclusionary legislation only when variables other than labor market conditions intervened, most notably those of race and ethnicity." Thus, encouraged by the "openly anti-Chinese" animus of the California Constitution of 1874, labor helped to pass "six federal Chinese Exclusion Acts between 1882 and 1904." The Gentleman's Agreement with Japan and the Asian Pacific Triangle of 1917 were also passed during this period. When pseudoscientific "theories" emerged that "questioned the moral, physical, and political fitness" of Southern and Eastern Europeans to enter the United States, labor aligned itself with the questioners, and in 1917 literacy tests and a head tax were imposed on immigrants over age sixteen; subsequently numerical quotas were imposed (Papademetriou and Miller 1983, pp. 8, 9).

From this time forward, anti-immigration fervor was heightened to the point that organized labor was able to ride on these sentiments and thus control the "main door" of immigration with little "expenditure of political capital." From 1917 onward, the anti-immigration coalition "was firmly in control." Labor was able to check the influx of Southern and Eastern Europeans by forming "alliances with those who questioned the moral, physical and political fitness of these groups" (Papademetriou and Miller 1983, p. 9).

In 1921, quotas were fixed at three percent of the total representation of each ethnic group in the 1910 census with the exception of those from the Western Hemisphere. When this formula was perceived as still allowing in too many "undesirables" from Southern and Eastern Europe, Congress passed the 1924 National Origins Act. As had been noted, "such a quota favored the countries of Western and Northern Europe because they had heretofore provided many more immigrants to the United States by 1890 than the nations of Eastern and Southern Europe, Asia, Africa, and Latin America" (Carrasco 1987, p. 3).

Organized labor's efforts had been "to restrict the level of immigration and then to secure special legislative protections for the domestic worker." To this end, organized labor won "the inclusion of a labor certification requirement in the McCarren–Walter Act of 1952, the country's basic immigration law" (Morris 1985, p. 15). A "labor certification requirement" meant that proof of need for foreign workers had to be demonstrated, for example, lack of domestic workers. Labor was able to strengthen this provision in the 1965 Immigration and Nationality Act. The House Judiciary Committee report noted that

This provision will adequately provide for the protection of American.labor against an influx of aliens entering the United States for the purpose of performing skilled or unskilled labor where the economy of individual localities is not capable of absorbing them at the time they desire to enter this country. (Morris 1985, p. 15)

However, labor's greatest victory came in shifting immigration policy away from replenishment of the work force to the theme of family reunification, refugee issues, and to the control of the use of temporary H-2 workers (Morris 1985, p. 16). Family reunification was to be given top priority, with preference shown in descending order to closeness of family relationship. Organized labor had argued in favor of putting the Department of Labor in an active role in the immigrant admissions decision-making process. The Department of Labor "succeeded in getting the wording of the labor certification procedure reversed from the previous law" (Roney, in Hesburgh, Staff Report 1981, pp. 328, 329). Under the 1965 adjustment, "an alien was excludable *unless* the Secretary of Labor determined there were not sufficient workers rather than *if* he or she determined there were sufficient workers." In addition, "non preference and Western Hemisphere immigrants were required to obtain individual labor certification following the 1965 changes in the law." Under the former labor certification procedure, the burden was on the Department of Labor to act retroactively. For example, if a consul noticed an employer recruiting more than twenty-five employees for a single area in a given year, the Department of Labor might look more closely at the specific labor market situation (Roney, in Hesburgh, Staff Report 1981, p. 329). These adjustments to the 1965 immigration legislation were clear victories for the interests of organized labor, but as we shall see in Chapter 3, their victories pale next to the bold initiative of capital in acquiring "needed" foreign workers.

The next chapter explores the elements of this third layer of ambivalence: finding supplies of temporary foreign workers, the triumph of agribusiness interests over labor, and the unique historical roots of undocumented immigration that is particular to the United States.

Chapter 3

The History of Undocumented Immigration in the United States

No democracy can flourish with an underclass outside of its basic laws.
Ray Marshall, Secretary of Labor, Carter administration

One of the central dynamics of immigration policy is that "for almost as long as the United States has sought to enforce general restrictions on immigration, there have been parallel legal steps to make formal exceptions for the admission of temporary foreign workers" (Briggs 1987, p. 995).

FINDING SUPPLIES OF "TEMPORARY" FOREIGN WORKERS: A THIRD LAYER OF AMBIVALENCE

This third layer of ambivalence represents agribusiness's attempts over the years to find pathways to "temporary" farm workers even in the midst of overall restrictive immigration policy. This avenue to temporary foreign workers needs to be elaborated on because it is the foundation of an understanding of how undocumented immigrants evolved into a social problem of such magnitude that legislative intervention through the Immigration Reform and Control Act of 1986 was required. The sheer number of "temporary" foreign labor programs in this century, when overall immigration policy was by and large restrictive, attests to the strength of capital's demands for foreign laborers even as organized labor protested vehemently. There were temporary worker programs from 1917 to 1922 and from 1942 to 1964; some would say, the continued "open" flow of undocumented workers who have entered the United States up until recent time with near impunity is in itself a kind of program. In 1917, capital was able to acquire "temporary" Mexican farm workers, miners, and railroad workers, and in 1942, the large-scale *bracero* program was initiated through an agreement between Mexico and the United States, which furnished Mexican farm workers for American agriculture (Papademetriou and Miller 1983, p. 8).

Even though regulations were set in place as early as 1942 governing the *bracero* program in order to protect American workers and their wages by guaranteeing minimum wage and workplace protections, enforcement was at a minimum. Fuchs maintains that "the bracero program was evidence of the willingness of the U.S. government to subsidize Southwest and California agriculture with cheap labor" (1990, p. 123).

Ellis Cose, in his 1992 book *A Nation of Strangers*, documents the collusion of the U.S. government with agribusiness around the use of undocumented immigrants. He describes how the "officially sanctioned" *bracero* workers became an illegal flow of Mexican workers who were so numerous that, according to the head of the Immigration and Naturalization Service in Los Angeles, their removal "particularly during harvest seasons, would have brought disaster to the agricultural enterprises employing them" (p. 93). This third layer of ambivalence, the need for temporary foreign workers, excluded undocumented immigrants with one hand and beckoned them forth with the other. U.S. borders to the south have remained remarkably porous, particularly throughout the nineteenth century when business was quite successful in wheedling from the executive and legislative branches of government concessions based on what many believed were "contrived labor shortages." A case in point is the transportation industry in the wake of the Civil War. "Capital actually secured legislation that included incentives and indirect public subsidies for labor procurement." Although this act was repealed four years later, it was an act "that set the tone both for a pattern of business practice of hiring foreign workers regardless of their legal status and for a pattern of impotence by successive labor organizations in checking this practice" (Papademetrious and Miller 1983, p. 8).

Over time a distinctly "American configuration" had evolved, according to Zolberg, which has structured our immigration policy into a "main gate/back door" system from the 1880s up to the present time. From this perspective Zolberg maintains that labor and immigration policies "particularly in the Southwest, have consistently resulted in conscientious human efforts . . . to keep wages low, to keep incomes depressed, and to keep unionism at a minimum by using waves of legal immigrants [from China, Japan, Mexico, and from Europe as well], bracero [from Mexico], border commuters [from

Mexico] and now illegal aliens [mainly from Mexico and the Caribbean but by no means exclusively so"] (in Papademetriou and Miller 1983, p. 9).

Briggs points to the most restrictive-to-date immigration legislation of 1917 as being also the point when the "first publicly sanctioned foreign-worker program for non immigrants was initiated." Agricultural employers from the southwest would press Congress for "temporary" workers from Western Hemisphere nations who were "otherwise inadmissible." Under the new statute, Mexican immigrants were excused from the head tax and literacy regulations. Enforcement of regulations was lax during this war period, and gradually some Mexican workers were allowed to branch out into nonfarm work. Several immigration scholars, including Briggs and Fuchs among others, refer to this 1917 program (which was extended to 1922) as "the first bracero program." It was terminated when its logic as a national defense policy could not be rationally maintained, when organized labor pressed its case in favor of citizen workers, and when many people began to contest the idea that there was a genuine labor shortage. More likely there were only avaricious employers who had become addicted to economic gains through a cheap, silent, and docile workforce (Briggs 1984, pp. 97, 98).

With the termination of this program and the uncertain economic times of the 1920s and 1930s, "temporary" labor immigration became less compelling for a time and pressure to return "temporary" and undocumented workers back to Mexico increased markedly. Directed specifically at Mexicans, the "Repatriation" campaign lasted from 1929 to 1939. The "Operation Wetback" program lasted from 1954 to 1958, as the United States removed, without formal deportation proceedings, millions of persons to Mexico, many of whom were American citizens (Carrasco 1987, p. 3).

However, World War II brought with it substantial pressure for foreign workers to subsidize what was described as severe labor shortages in agribusiness. Once again, therefore, in 1942 the Mexican government agreed to a new, large-scale *bracero* temporary worker program that would provide migrant workers for the American agricultural sector. It lasted until 1947 and was utilized again in 1951 to 1964. When the program peaked in 1956, there were nearly a half million temporary workers in the United States per year (Briggs 1987, p. 998). In total, from 1942 to 1965 approximately four to five million temporary workers were admitted to the United States (Forbes, in Hesburgh, Staff Report 1981, p. 469). Interestingly, the *bracero* program was not part of overall immigration policy but was instead part of general congressional legislation. Under these programs protections such as wage controls, medical insurance, free housing, and transportation, while legislated, remained "inadequately, if at all provided by U.S. employers" (Briggs 1987, p. 998). What this program did was expose Mexican workers to wage and working conditions far superior to those in Mexico. Thus it "institutionalized the process whereby many former bracero workers having been exposed to the United States labor market continued to seek work in the U.S. in subsequent years, as illegal aliens after the bracero programs ended" (Briggs 1987, pp. 998, 999).

Walter Fogel in his article "Immigrants and the Labor Market," maintains that the *bracero* program contributed to the abiding U.S. undocumented immigration problem in two unique ways: "It set in motion a heavy flow of illegal immigrants from Mexico during the early 1950s," a flow requiring para-military deportations of dubious legality carried out in the 1950s; and Fogel asserts, "labor flows once authorized under the bracero program became illegal immigration after the program ended and continue today at much increased levels" (Papademetriou and Miller 1983, p. 74).

The 1952 Immigration and Nationality Act created two categories of noncitizens entering the United States: immigrants or nonimmigrants. Within the new classification system of twelve separate categories was the provision for an H-2 program. This program provided the category "other temporary workers." Theoretically, H-2 workers were supposed to enter the United States only for work that was also temporary in nature and only when it could be certified by the Department of Labor that "unemployed citizens and permanent resident aliens cannot be found to perform the needed job" (Briggs 1987, p. 999). In this model, prevailing wages and benefits were to be paid to the H-2 workers.

In practice, controversy developed around several practices that Briggs indicates were "considered unfair and illegal if applied to citizen workers" (1984, p. 97). Under the H-2 program, employers did not have to pay social security or unemployment compensation. If the H-2 workers were citizens, of course, they would be required by law to pay both of these. Beyond this, because employers could request by name 60 percent of their current H-2 workers for the next year, the H-2 workers were cast into a very imbalanced, dependent relationship with the employer. In this climate of trying to please their employer and compete with other H-2 workers in order to be selected, it is not surprising that H-2 workers are reported to be "hard working and diligent" (Briggs 1984, p. 107). Temporary worker programs were begun in wartime because of genuine labor shortages but continued long past their original purpose into periods of peace and high unemployment. Briggs makes the point that "conditions under which foreign workers are employed seem only to be beneficial to the self-interest of the employers" who find in foreign workers a "docile" labor force that is "almost impossible to unionize" and "who can be treated in an arbitrary way with impunity" (1987, p. 1001).

Problems with this program include the question raised by Papademetriou and Miller: Who decides "when a shortage is real and when is it contrived?" A second question, already alluded to, revolves around the nature of the relationship that is created between the H-2 worker and the single employer to whom the H-2 worker is tied to during his time as an H-2 worker. This uneven, "one-sided power relationship" suggests to some a modern form of "indentured servitude" (1983, p. 15).

Malvern and Frederick in their study on employer attitudes in San Diego, California found that "employers did not fear that they would go out of business if they had to pay competitive wages for citizen workers or that they could not find available citizen workers at prevailing wage rates. Rather, employers simply believed they could make more profits by paying lower wages as the result of hiring foreign workers than if they had to seek citizen workers" (in Briggs 1987, p. 1001).

Although visas for H-2 workers peaked in 1969 at over 69,000, on a yearly basis, they average between 25,000 to 35,000. Roughly half, over the last number of years, have been agricultural workers. The rest find themselves in Florida in the sugar cane fields, in upstate New York or Virginia as apple pickers, or in Maine as loggers (Briggs 1987, p. 1000). Since the termination of *bracero* programs, southwest growers have turned to undocumented immigrants to pick their fruits and vegetables. The general sense was that approval of H-2 workers by the government moved too slowly to meet the demand for workers of seasonal and perishable goods. Various attempts to broaden the H-2 program can be seen as ways to "ween Southwestern growers away from their dependence on illegal immigrants whose employment would be illegal if employer sanctions were adopted" (Briggs 1987, p. 1004).

As the focus of immigration reform in the 1970s and 1980s began to zero in on slamming the back door shut in terms of cutting off the flow of undocumented immigrants, the issue of extending and broadening the H-2 program to make foreign workers accessible to employers surfaced once again. As with the *bracero* program, H-2 programs exposed foreign workers to the U.S. job market and therefore paved the way for undocumented migration when the temporary foreign worker program ended or when the foreign worker was not chosen to continue as an H-2 worker.

Milton Morris in his book, *Immigration: The Beleaguered Bureaucracy*, succinctly summarizes how organized labor's fears were somewhat mollified by the 1965 immigration law's emphasis on family unification rather than labor force augmentation. Still, the legislation contained a temporary worker program which heightened "concerns about continued use of temporary seasonal workers and the sharp rise in illegal immigration during the 1970s . . . [rekindling] labor's fear of extensive job losses." Indeed, the decade-long effort to enact IRCA was based on the "belief that illegal immigrants displace domestic workers, depress wages, and contribute to poor working conditions." While major disagreements still exist among researchers, analysts, and policy makers about the effects of undocumented immigration on the labor market, a momentum had been created based on the belief that attempts to control illegal immigration were indeed "job creating efforts" (1985, pp. 15, 16, 17).

The continued mounting tension regarding the economic effect of undocumented immigration on the labor market was reflective of America's "ongoing ambivalence: immigrants are wanted for their cheap labor but are feared as a potential economic burden" (Sellers 1984, p. 158). For Fuchs (1992) it is a matter of "how schizophrenic the U.S. has been about immigrants—wanting them and fearing them at the same time."

ECONOMIC IMPACT:
JOB DISPLACEMENT AND COMPETITION

It is clear that public debate about immigration reform prior to the enactment of IRCA rested on the assumption "that the country was seriously threatened by an unprecedented surge" of undocumented immigration (Morris 1985, p. 6). A second interrelated assumption was that undocumented immigration had a negative impact on the economic, social, and political well-being of the nation.

Colorado Governor Richard Lamm, arguing in 1981 that the country needed to control the flow of new immigrants, declared that immigration was at its highest level to date and further stated that immigration "aggravates our social epidemic of unemployment and scarcity. . . . It is usually not recognized but the nation's largest number of immigrants came not in 1911 or 1963 but in 1980—808,000 legal immigrants and over one million apprehensions of illegals—ten times the number in the early 1960s" (Pedraza-Bailey 1985, p. 165). Briggs points out that there are severe problems with using the number of illegal immigrants apprehended as an indicator of the magnitude of the problem because the same undocumented immigrants may have crossed the border, been detained several times, and crossed again the same year (1984, p. 132).

Nonetheless it is clear that emotion escalated as attention was focused on the problem of immigration in general interchanged with concern over the influx of immigrants unsanctioned by law. Speaking prior to perestroika, William F. Colby, then director of the Central Intelligence Agency (CIA), had termed the flow of Mexican undocumented immigrants across the country's southern border "a greater threat to the future of the United States than the Soviet Union" (Crewdson 1983, p. 17).

The Environmental Fund (TEF), a restrictionist interest group, assured its readers that "the border patrol knows that for every illegal alien who is apprehended perhaps four go uncaught" and that "those who are caught eventually get in." A second tireless immigration restrictionist group, Zero Population Growth (ZPG), warned that "one-fourth to one-half of the nation's population growth is attributable to immigration." A third restrictionist group, the Federation of American Immigration Reform (FAIR), indicated that "the number of illegal aliens who had come here over the past decade had reached four million" (Crewdson 1983, p. 99).

The problem with these assertions is that there is no credible evidence that they are true. There is also no credible evidence that any of these claims are untrue. Immigration scholar Laurence Fuchs, past executive director of the

Select Commission on Immigration and Refugee Policy dismissed existing research that attempted to document the numbers of illegal immigrants in the United States with this admonition: "Gossip about gossip is still gossip" (in Crewdson 1983, p. 98).

Among the questions that the phenomenon of undocumented immigration had raised are the same ones that have always preoccupied Americans in times of economic downspins: Were undocumented immigrants taking jobs from U.S. citizens? Are undocumented immigrants using tax-generated public funds through their use of welfare and public social services? And finally, will undocumented and legal immigrants turn U.S. cities into culturally and linguistically isolated and potentially hostile enclaves (Crewdson 1983, p. 19)?

The increase in the numbers of undocumented immigrants apprehended by the INS gave credence to public concern. Whether the increase in numbers was due to increased enforcement or simply an increase in the number attempting to enter the United States remains less clear. As shown in Glazer's statistics on apprehensions, 1983 was noteworthy in that the number of undocumented immigrants detained reached an all time high of over 1.2 million:

1965	110,371
1975	756,919
1977	1,033,427
1978	1,047,687
1979	1,069,400
1983	1,248,000 (adapted from Glazer 1985, p. 143)

In the public hearings across the nation held by the Select Commission in their study of immigration issues, Theodore Hesburgh, chairperson, reported, "one issue has emerged as most pressing . . . the problem of undocumented/illegal migration. The message is clear. . . . Most United States citizens believe the half open door of undocumented/illegal migration should be closed" (Hesburgh, Final Report 1981, p. 35). The commission heard terms such as "uncontrolled hemorrhage of people," "flaunting of the law," and "exploitation of illegal aliens" (p. 35).

Evidence about the numbers and impact of undocumented aliens has always been scarce, inconclusive, and even contradictory. Reimers reports that "spectacular raids" on undocumented aliens by the Immigration and Naturalization Service (INS) "sharply increased apprehensions and growing media coverage—sometimes sensational—all contributed to heightened political and public awareness of undocumented aliens after 1968, especially during the 1970s and 1980s just as the nation was experiencing inflation and slumps in the economy." In 1972, *United States News and World Report* published the following headline: "Surge of Illegal Immigrants across American Borders."

The article stated, "Never have so many aliens swarmed illegally into the United States—millions, moving across the nation. For government, they are becoming a costly headache." Two years later, the *New York Times* spoke of a "silent invasion," intimating that one million undocumented aliens alone inhabited the metropolitan area. The *New Orleans Times-Picayune*, reporting on an INS estimate of undocumented aliens, announced, "Illegal Aliens: They invade the U.S. 8.2 million strong" (Reimers 1985, pp. 213, 214).

Estimates of the numbers of undocumented aliens residing unlawfully within the United States will probably always remain just that: estimates. Because the undocumented are in the country illegally, they take great pains to remain invisible, with no records of who they are or where they are. In looking into the questions of numbers of undocumented aliens in 1978, the Select Commission on Immigration and Refugee Policy received permission from the Bureau of the Census to have their chief demographers, Jacob S. Seigal, Jeffrey S. Passel, and J. Gregory Robinson, review the literature on the subject and report to the commission (Forbes, in Hesburgh, Staff Report 1981, p. 480). The demographers noted the "amount of controversy," the "lack of hard data," and "the methodological errors" in the various studies and decided that "no reliable count was available" (Reimers 1985, p. 215). They concluded,

Although the numbers of illegal residents in the United States remains uncertain, the authors are willing to make some inferences from the available studies with regard to the possible magnitude of the numbers. They offer the following cautious speculations. The total number of illegal residents in the United States for some recent year, such as 1978, is almost certainly below 6 million and may be substantially less, possibly only 3.5 to 5 million. The existing estimates of illegal residents based on empirical studies simply do not support the claim that there are very many millions (i.e. over 6 million) of unlawful residents in the United States. (Reimers 1985, pp. 215–216)

Reflecting on this same literature, demographer Charles B. Keely echoes the same conclusion. He estimates that the "number of illegal migrants around 1973–1975 to be in the lower end of the 4 to 12 million range used by former INS Commissioner, Leonard Chapman" (Forbes, in Hesburgh, Staff Report 1981, p. 482). It is easy to see how these same broad ranges of estimates could be used to bolster arguments on either side of the undocumented alien question, with the ability to choose either the upper or lower limit, depending on the specific point of view to be driven home.

Simon indicated that "the labor market effects of illegal immigrants, are similar to, and an inextricable part of, the effects of all immigrants" (1989, p. 298). Therefore, the studies on the impact of legal immigration considered earlier are appropriate for discussion of undocumented immigration as well. Still, some studies, using data on undocumented immigrants, address themselves specifically to the undocumented population. In one such piece of empirical research, Bean, Lowell, and Taylor studied the impact of the undocumented portion of Mexican immigrants on legal U.S workers in southwestern metropolitan labor markets. The labor force groups used in the study "were (a) undocumented Mexicans, (b) legal, and (c) native-born, Mexican-origin males, (d) black males, (e) non-Mexican origin white males, and (f) females." The most general findings of the study were that "illegal Mexican immigrants are negative upon white males' wages (substitution) and positive (complementarity) upon females' wages." The authors note that the "magnitudes of the effects are hard to predict" and "not very sizeable." They conclude, "The concern that undocumented immigration may be depressing the earnings of native-born workers does not appear to be borne out by these results" (in Simon 1989, pp. 236, 237).

An empirical study by Barton Smith and Robert Newman on "Depressed Wages Along the U.S.–Mexican Border" found that in areas near the border, annual income is $684 less than metropolitan areas away from the border. This wage differential was found to be "slightly higher for Mexican Americans and for unskilled workers." The authors "believe that these wage differentials may be caused in part by undocumented/illegal migration," but conclude that "if migration from Mexico is having a negative impact on wages along the border, it is not as severe as many contended" (Forbes, in Hesburgh, Staff Report 1981, p. 509).

The final report of the Select Commission on Immigration and Refugee Policy concluded that, similar to the findings of most economists, "the extent of competition between native workers and migrants depends on the degree to which they have similar job skills." Undocumented immigrants tend to be young and unskilled. It is more than likely that young, less-skilled native-born workers "will be most adversely affected by their presence." The Select Commission summed up by noting that "although the effect of undocumented/illegal immigration on the U.S. labor force is not quantifiable, it is apparent that the continuing flow of undocumented workers across U.S. borders has certainly contributed to the displacement of some U.S. workers and the depression of some U.S. wages" (Hesburgh, Staff Report 1981, p. 41).

Michael Piore in his book *Birds of Passage* alluded to the same fact, that is, that the impact of undocumented workers falls on "native-born disadvantaged workers who are themselves trapped in the secondary market." Piore suggests that the way out for low-skilled U.S. workers trapped in the secondary market is training and other types of education to lift them out of this market into the primary market and therefore foster their "upward mobility" (1979, p. 168).

Two experimental projects in 1977 that studied the results of removing undocumented immigrants from their jobs are of interest. In the first experiment, "A Study of the Socio-Economic Impact of Illegal Aliens," 2,154 undocumented immigrants were removed from their jobs; the California State Human Resources Agency then attempted to fill the vacated jobs with U.S. native-born workers, but to no avail. In explaining the results the County of San Diego Human Resources Agency noted several reasons for the failure: the first reason was that most "employers paid less than the minimum wage rate"; second, "the job categories were not appealing to the local resident (a matter of prestige)"; and third, applicants were put off by the low wages along with the difficulty of some jobs, and the long hours that were required (Simon 1989, p. 299).

On November 16, 1975, the INS in San Diego began what they referred to as the "Employment Cooperation Program" as a second experimental project. The program helped employers identify undocumented workers, "remove them from the payroll, and fill the job slots with local unemployed residents." In all, over the period from November 1975 to April 1976, 340 undocumented immigrants were identified and their jobs terminated. The jobs held by these 340 undocumented workers "were in the areas of hotel maintenance, food handling, food processing, laundrymen and operative." The highest numbers were in hotel-related jobs (160). One hundred and nineteen were in light manufacturing, 41 in food process work, and 20 in general services. Eighty-one percent of undocumented workers were earning $2 or less per hour. The hourly wage ranges of the vacated jobs were from $1.75 to $7.05. The results indicate that the "Employment Cooperation Program" did indeed fill all 340 vacancies. However, the newly created job opportunities were not filled by local residents as had been expected. Instead, 90 percent of the job slots were filled by "commuter workers from Baja California, Mexico" (Simon 1989, pp. 229, 230).

Although these experiments are not generalizable or conclusive, they do support the view that many of the jobs that the undocumented hold would not be filled by U.S. citizens in the absence of undocumented workers. Overall, the debate over whether undocumented workers displace U.S. native-born workers has suffered a certain lack of precision in terms of long-term versus short-term labor market consequences in relation to the flow of undocumented immigration. As already noted most economists would agree that the "extent of competition depends on the degree to which they have similar job skills" (Hesburgh, Final Report 1981, p. 41). Added to this there is a lack of precision in terms of aggregate versus regional and local effects and a pattern of ignoring short-term and local displacement. One immigration scholar, Mines, "denies that displacement, as such, occurs," but speaks instead of "employer abandonment of veteran citizen workers" in favor of "recent immigrants" as a means of keeping labor costs low. The point is made that "although nation-wide immigration may have created more jobs than it is removing, this fact is of little solace to individual 'abandoned' workers who are often poor and with low job skills" (in Simcox 1988, p. 33). In sum, it can be said with a fair amount of accuracy that the evidence furnished by research is "inconclusive" about whether the presence of undocumented workers displace native-born workers or depress their wages. What can be stated is that the impact of un-documented immigrant workers "on labor markets is locality—and industry-specific" (Bean, Schmandt, and Weintraub 1989, p. 204).

COSTS TO PUBLIC SERVICES

One researcher, Forbes, tells us that attempts to measure the impact of undocumented immigrants on public social services such as cash assistance and medical and educational services is every bit as difficult as assessing the labor market and wage impact of the undocumented. One of the reasons that this is the case is that in order to measure the effect of the undocumented on social services, several other factors would need to be taken into account. Among them are the following: "their contribution through taxes to social services, their own utilization of services, and the effects that labor market displacement and wage depression may have on the use of services by U.S. citizens and permanent resident aliens" (Forbes, in Hesburgh, Staff Report 1981, pp. 519, 520).

The argument is made that undocumented immigrants use public social services for which they do not pay and are therefore a burden on U.S. taxpayers. Emergency medical costs for indigent undocumented immigrants are often cited in this regard (Forbes, in Hesburgh, Staff Report 1981, pp. 519, 520). The underlying issue here is "the question of payment" which draws us into the question of whether the undocumented are a local or federal responsibility.

Throughout the 1970s the prevailing concern was that social service costs were rising disproportionately because of escalating use by undocumented immigrants (Simcox 1988, p. 37). Although little factual information was available, credence could be given to this notion because, in the past, there had been a time when there were no barriers to participation in public social services (Ainsworth 1986, p. 40).

However, by the early 1970s and into the early 1980s, a number of federal laws and regulations were passed that barred undocumented immigrants from most federal programs; this included Supplemental Security Insurance (SSI), Aid to Families with Dependent Children (AFDC), food stamps, unemployment compensation, and student financial loans (Simcox 1988, p. 37). Undocumented immigrants cannot participate in Medicaid or housing assistance. Even legal resident aliens were restricted in their use of social welfare programs through legislation in the 1970s that required sponsors of legal immigrants to use their own financial resources for the social welfare needs of those they were sponsoring for the first three years of residency. It was during this period that screening legal aliens to discern their "likelihood of becoming a public charge" was initiated (Simcox 1988, p. 37). As we shall see in later chapters, this phrase became imbedded in the minds of the undocumented as the main barrier to becoming legalized in the United States and accounts for some of their fear of using public programs.

Undocumented immigrants are not eligible for public benefits, including unemployment insurance and social security, but they pay for these programs through taxes and payroll deductions if they are employed. The problem is that roughly two-thirds of the tax dollars paid by legal and undocumented immigrants go directly to the federal level while, the state and local governments pay for most of the health, education, and social service costs. Beyond this, over the last decade or so, the federal government has drastically pulled back funds earmarked for programs to assist the undocumented.

As Wayne Cornelius points out:

It is clear that discussion of the "social welfare costs" of illegal migration which fails to take account of the migrants' contributions to tax revenues provide a grossly distorted view of the "burden" imposed on the United States by the migrants. All available evidence suggests that they are subsidizing the system rather than draining it (Abrams 1984, p. 117)

Use of welfare by undocumented immigrants in the North and Houston Study (Simon 1989, p. 289) broke down into the following percentages:

Used free public hospital or clinic	5.0 percent
Collected one or more weeks of unemployment insurance	3.9 percent
Have children in public schools	3.7 percent
Participated in U.S.–funded job training program	1.4 percent
Secured food stamps	1.3 percent
Secured welfare payments	0.5 percent

Simon indicates that, "taken together," the overall impact of undocumented immigrants on the public coffers is positive, even if the picture differs "in a particular local or state jurisdiction." Though undocumented and legal immigrants "may cost a specific state or city more" in services than the locality receives in taxes, this is not true for the community as a whole "when federal and social security contributions are included" (1989, pp. 292–293).

REACHING A LEVEL OF INTOLERANCE:
THE VARIABLE OF RACE AND ETHNICITY

An August 25, 1986 issue of *Time* quoted Theodore H. White's description of undocumented immigrants in the following excerpt:

The border patrol (in the San Diego sector) picked up 4,000 lawless migrants back in 1965; in 1985 the number was 421,000. . . . The farmers, wanderers, smugglers, pregnant mothers, drug peddlers do not seem like the stuff of crises, but they are. (In Simcox 1988, p. 1)

Alan Simpson, who went on to become the cosponsor of the 1986 IRCA legislation, "had claimed that Mexican immigration threatens a territorial and cultural 'Quebec-ization' of the United States" (Cockcroft 1986, p. 143).

Clearly, as Portes and Kincaid point out, "The casting of new immigrant groups as scapegoats in time of social and economic distress has been a recurrent phenomenon in American History" (1985, p. 74). More pointed, however, is the insight that "nowadays, a latent xenophobia is often aroused by Hispanic migrants, particularly if they are illegal immigrants from Mexico and Central America" ("California Indicts the Immigration Law" 1990, p. 163). Indeed, the immigration debate, far from being exclusively about numbers, is also a "veiled discussion about the future ethnic make-up of the United States" (Ocasio 1995, p. 17).

The Domestic Council on Illegal Immigrants reported that the main sources of undocumented immigrants to the United States around the late 1970s and early 1980s were from the following countries: Mexico, Haiti, Dominican Republic, Jamaica, Guatemala, Colombia, Peru, Ecuador, Philippines, Korea, Thailand, Greece, India, Iran, and Nigeria. It is interesting to note that except for Guatemala, Thailand, and Ecuador, these countries were also the leading source of legal immigration during that period (Bryce-Leporte 1982, p. 72).

The impact of the 1965 immigration law can be clearly seen in the legal admissions of these diverse ethnic and racial groups that had previously been excluded from entry by law. Reactions to new legal immigrants and undocumented immigrants may well reflect this "visible" shift in the ethnicity and race of the newer immigration stream. The 1980 refugee legislation failed to anticipate the huge numbers seeking asylum. By 1983 there were 170,000 asylum seekers: two-thirds from Cuba but also large numbers from El Salvador, Haiti, Iran, and Nicaragua (Simcox 1988, p. 55). Over the decades of the 1970s and 1980s, talk of "regaining control of United States borders" in the Congress and the White House had been seen by some observers as transparent code words for keeping Mexicans out of the United States.

Immigration scholars Bean, Schmandt, and Weintraub contend that reports on the size of the undocumented population in the United States "have increasingly proven to be smaller than many observers have speculated." As noted earlier, this is also the case with regard to studies "on the labor market impact that have consistently found small effects of immigrants (both legal and undocumented) on wages and earnings of other labor force groups." Bean and colleagues add, "Ironically, however, public perceptions have often run in the opposite direction. How can this discrepancy [between perception and evidence] be explained?" (1989, p. 105).

Immigration researcher Charles Keely suggests that "the bottom line" question in immigration matters "seems to be whether the United States is receiving 'unmeltable ethnics.'" What is at issue is the question of whether the new immigrants will "outbreed" the native born and whether they will continue to enter the country in such numbers as to change "the nature and character" of American society. Keely believes that the real issue, "if one speaks honestly, is what proportion [of America] will be Hispanic and secondarily, Asian." He contends further that "the ethnic composition issue appears to revolve around whether immigrants are 'too different' and therefore will not only not be assimilated, but may even make Americans 'more like' them." He makes the point that when social discourse is filled with words like "invasion," "hordes," "inundated," and "floods," the implication is that destruction lies just around the corner" (in Bean, Schmandt, and Weintraub 1989, pp. 172, 173).

Gordenker situating U.S. immigration policy in an international setting shares Keely's concern: "At the bottom of the debate on numbers, limits, and the 'desirable' ethnic composition of migrant flows to any advanced industrialized democracy is a basic concern with the future ethnic, cultural and linguistic profile of the society in question." He goes on to say that "although American concern over this is often couched in perfectly neutral terms, the fear is of an unduly Hispanic United States fifty or a hundred years from now." Gordenker speaks plainly in referring to what he calls "a usually latent but increasingly open sentiment of 'Hispanaphobia'" (in Papademetriou and Miller 1983, p. 292).

Michael LeMay in his book *From Open Door to Dutch Door: An Analysis of Immigration Policy since 1920*, states that a "study released by the Population Reference Bureau estimates that the Hispanic population will reach 47 million by the year 2020, displacing blacks as the nation's largest minority group" (1987, p. 125). Gordenker makes clear that the "dominance of Hispanics in both legal and clandestine immigration flows" will surely influence the future direction of the country, whether in foreign policy or in the linguistic or cultural mix. What needs to be avoided, he explains, is "the value judgment" that America will be the worst for it (1983, p. 294).

Laurence Fuchs pointed out in the SCIRP staff report that America is "the first [country] in history whose national identity has been shaped, not by race, ethnicity or religion, but rather by shared political values and ideals" (in Hesburgh, Staff Report 1981, p. 110). Therefore, as Keely notes, "to ask what holds America together is a serious question" and not necessarily "a bigoted one" in and of itself. The problem, according to the analysis of Keely is that "the question is not being raised in a non-bigoted way." He maintains that contemporary questions "on the size and composition of today's immigration" are raised without an historical context and without reference to other countries' experiences. In actuality the United States, as a nation of immigrants, "has fewer foreign-born than Argentina, Venezuela, France, Germany, England or Switzerland. Other traditionally immigrant countries such as Canada, Australia and New Zealand have two to three times the proportion of foreigners than America does" (1989, p. 171). In fact, immigration statistics as of 1998 placed the numbers of foreign-born legal immigrants at 9.3 percent of the overall U.S. population. In other words, one U.S. resident in ten was foreign born. In 1999, undocumented immigration was estimated to be one percent of the overall population ("One US Resident in 10 Is Now Foreign Born" 1999, p. 37). According to the 1980 census, the United States had about 6.2 percent foreign-born persons within its borders. Keely points out that given the "nation's history of past absorption of immigrants and the experience of other countries, there has been no evidence to suggest that countries have fallen apart socially or culturally as a result of immigration." Further, he suggests that "an objection to having too many foreigners seems to be primarily a matter of taste or preference [rather than] of demonstrated economic and social problems" (1989, p. 171).

Paraphrasing Gunnar Myrdal, Gordenker insists that "the greatest threat to national unity" is not the cultural diversity offered through new groups of immigrants, but rather, "the pervasive and historical racism of American society." Gordenker notes further that "the myth of cultural pluralism usually works well only when race does not intrude as a variable" (1983, p. 295).

The question to be pursued in the next section, among others, is whether this variable of racism, this "dead hand of the past," found its way into the lengthy deliberations on the legalization and employer sanctions provisions of IRCA and with what effect for the enactment of the 1986 immigration legislation.

Thus far it can be said that the gradual escalation of the issue of undocumented immigration into a full-blown social problem requiring political intervention began in 1965 with the admission of legal immigrants from various racial and ethnic groups heretofore excluded by law. With an increase in the volume of legal immigration and refugees and a perceived increase in undocumented immigration largely from the same ethnic groups as legal immigrants, the stage was set for an emotionally volatile debate on the same issues traditionally raised about new immigrants, but with one important difference. This time the debate raged around an easy, silent target: immigrants in the country unsanctioned by law. In spite of inconclusive data on the volume and the social and economic impact of undocumented immigrants on American society, a crescendo had been reached. In this atmosphere an easily scapegoated group such as undocumented immigrants could stand in the place of what may have been the real target: racially and ethnically diverse new, "unmeltable" legal immigrants. These new arrivals had been permitted entry into the country when for the first time the United States decided "to cast a blind eye on the world" in terms of racial and ethnic differences. In a final irony or ambivalence toward newcomers, the nation that had beckoned them forth had now begun to reject them.

INTEREST GROUP POLITICS AND
THE LEGISLATIVE PROCESS

The most potent and durable force driving immigration policies over the years has not been ethnic and racial discrimination by itself but rather in combination with economic need as embodied in the central and countervailing positions of organized labor over and against capital and business interests. Time and again, various business interests in favor of unrestricted immigration have battled organized labor's pressure to restrict immigration.

In shaping policy agendas, Morris contends that "the attitudes of the general public have been less influential in shaping immigration policy than those of a much smaller segment of the population consisting of activists operating in pressures [*sic*] groups" (1985, p. 27). Interest groups or stakeholders have been defined as "individuals or groups who either have some input into decision making about a social problem, or are affected by policy decisions on that problem" (Majchrzak 1984, p. 28). Immigration scholar David North (1983) has identified some of the interest groups that have aligned themselves on either side of the debate over open or restrictive immigration policy. Restrictionists have included "many liberals, conservatives, taxpayer groups, population-control advocates, ethnic and racial bigots, environmentalists, law-and-order people, organized labor, and the black leadership." In contrast, anti-restrictionists include agricultural employers and "secondary market employers of illegals, the State Department, the Mexican government, the church, the Hispanic leadership, civil libertarians, the Left and the immigration bar." These diverse groups have been united in their support for open or restricted immigration policies respectively, but the reason for their support can and does vary widely. This is indeed a case of politics making strange bedfellows. Labor, in particular, has exhibited a marked degree of ambivalence over the years on legal and undocumented immigration (in Papademetriou and Miller 1983, p. 27).

Morris has divided the most prominent interest groups opposed to expanding immigration over the past century into three broad categories: (1) patriotic-nationalistic organizations such as "the major veteran's groups, the Allied Patriotic Societies, the Daughters of the American Revolution, and the Liberty Lobby"; (2) labor organizations such as "the American Federation of Labor (AFL) before its merger with the Congress of Industrial Organizations (CIO)"; and (3) "the recently formed growth limitation organizations such as Zero Population Growth (ZPG) and the Federation for American Immigration Reform (FAIR)." Collectively, these interest groups "have articulated the many fears and prejudices that have helped to shape" U.S. immigration policy over the years. However, there is great diversity in the interests of these various groups, and some interest groups have all but disappeared in terms of their impact on major public debates on immigration policy. After the overthrow of the national origins system in 1965, the patriotic-nationalist groups that opposed liberal immigration policies because some ethnic and racial groups were undesirable as immigrants lost favor in public debate. However, newer groups have come into existence which while eschewing the cultural and racial discrimination of the patriotic-nationalistic groups, argue for curbs on immigration because of its alleged "adverse effects on society and the environment." The most active anti-immigration organizations are ZPG, FAIR, and The Environmental Fund. The chairman of ZPG, John H. Taunton, summed up the philosophy of the group at the 1975 congressional hearings on the demographic effects of immigration when he testified, "Since immigration can significantly affect population growth, an immigration policy must be integrated into any such population stabilization program" (Morris 1985, p. 28).

Taunton commented in 1975 that immigration alone would add roughly 56 million to the projected 258 million population growth for the year 2000. (Actual figures for the U.S. population in the year 2000 was 270 million in total, with 10% new immigrants and approximately 1% undocumented immigrants.) Taunton's next comment contained a veiled threat to the status quo in America: "It is probably through illegal immigration that the citizens of the developed countries are most directly going to experience the population growth of less developed countries" (in Morris 1985, p. 28).

Other long-term opponents of expanded immigration have more and more come to adopt the arguments of ZPG and Federation for Immigration Reform on the dangers of population growth. Simon makes it clear that even when addressing themselves to the question of legal immigration, interest groups such as FAIR, ZPG, and The Environmental Fund continuously stress the theme that the nation is "being overwhelmed by a horde of illegal Mexican entrants" and that we "have lost control of our borders." Conner, a past executive director of FAIR, alluded to "powerful economic forces that are benefiting from illegal immigration and presumably are the cause of its continuation" (in Simon 1989, p. 278).

In general, interest groups aligned as opponents of expanded immigration link their concerns to the economic reversals that the country had experienced in the mid-1970s and 1980s. They argued "that the intensified pressures on government to cope with the rising costs of basic services indicate that the United States is unable to absorb large numbers of immigrants" (Morris 1985, p. 29).

Among the groups supportive of liberal immigration policies are ethnic groups representative of the broader, major ethnic groups in the United States, liberal religious organizations, liberal, progressive and human rights groups, and some labor groups. Specific groups include the ACLU, the AFL-CIO, the National Association of Manufacturers, and Americans for Democratic Action. Again, "while these groups are united in their support for expanded immigration policies, they have differed in their reasons for this support" (Morris 1985, p. 29).

In immigration debate prior to passage of IRCA, the most vocal advocates of open immigration policies were the Mexican–American Legal Defense and Education Fund (MALDEF) and the League of United Latin American Citizens (LULAC). Simcox indicates that several "Hispanic activists who had been raised in the confrontational politics of the 1960's began gaining leadership roles" in both MALDEF and LULAC. They carefully monitor immigration policies for signs of discrimination against Hispanics (1988, p. 6).

African Americans have been the newest interest group to join the immigration debate. The Congressional Black Caucus aligned itself with Hispanic groups in a proimmigration stance in opposition to racially discriminatory refugee policies toward Haitian boat people. On the other hand, as Simcox reports, black advocacy groups such as the National Association for the Advancement of Colored People (NAACP) and the Urban League worried about job displacement of African Americans by new immigrant groups, and therefore support efforts to curb undocumented immigration (1988, p. 6).

Agricultural and small- and medium-sized business groups have generally supported liberal immigration policies because immigrants are seen as supplements to the domestic workforce. Growers and manufacturers believe that such policies not only strengthen the workforce but also increase "the demand for goods and services." Growers in the northeast and southern United States tote immigration as the solution for shortages of agricultural workers (Morris 1985, p. 31).

Organized labor has historically fought against liberal immigration policies. However, this interest group has more than one voice and more than one position on immigration. Early on, the AFL prior to its merger with the CIO had supported the literacy test, the quota system, the retention of the Chinese exclusion laws, and the McCarren–Walter Act. However, the Congress of Industrialized Organizations (CIO) has historically supported liberal immigration policies. A CIO representative testified before the Truman Commission on Immigration in 1951:

The CIO realizes from past experience that immigration is automatically checked in periods of unemployment while it rises in periods of prosperity; that in the past, immigrants contributed in innumerable ways to the wealth and well-being of this country . . . that new blood in industry, agriculture, business, and the professions enriches our national life; and that the best and most enlightened thought on this subject opposes arbitrary, prejudicial, and superficial legislation to curb immigration into the United States. (Morris 1985, pp. 31–32)

"With the merger between the AFL and the CIO, the CIO's position was ... out." The new AFL-CIO remained a staunch opponent of temporary worker (H-2) programs and supported "strong measures to curb undocumented immigration but it also supports liberal legal immigration policy" (Morris 1985, p. 32).

Sassen notes that next to these interest groups on either side of the immigration debate, we must also place "the hierarchies of power and influence within the state [nation] that are being reconfigured by the furthering of economic globalization." Increasingly this includes the posture of a particular nation toward international agreements on human rights (1999, p. 22).

As Paul Light points out in his study of Congress and the Social Security system when he speaks of the legislative process, "the American system is not well designed to set priorities among competing goals." He explains that neither the Congress nor the presidency are "immune" to the "meddling" of interest groups. Light says that increasingly as the White House and Congress reach out to interest groups, "interest groups reach further into the Presidency and the Congress." Another direction in which interest groups reach is into the public in a process that can, at times, exploit public fears. Whereas in the past Congress was "once partly shielded from interest groups by strong committees and closed doors," it "now operates within a highly decentralized subcommittee system" and under the glare of television cameras. In this newer mode, "power has been dispersed to all 535 members" of Congress. In this sense, Light indicates that each congressperson has become "a legislative powerbroker. Now there are 535 power centers with their 'staffs' and their 'subcommittee assignments'" (1985, pp. 4, 5, 14). Mayhew contends that for any given piece of legislation from introduction to enactment, legislation is subject to debate and compromise in subcommittees, on the floors of both houses, with the administration, and with public interest groups, lobbyists, and constituents. He stresses that "except for the most popular or the most mundane of proposals, the consensus required for passing legislation demands compromise." William Greider speaks thus of congressional lawmaking in his article "The Grand Bazaar: Living with the Federal Bureaucracy": "Congress, after all, does not really enact laws in most areas—it proposes subjects for bargaining in the bazaar" (both in Williams 1980, pp. 45, 50).

The complexity of the role of interest groups in the legislative process as it relates to contemporary immigration policy is compounded by the fact that various pressure groups have focused on different immigration issues. For example, while some interest groups have concentrated broadly on whether immigration should be more or less restricted, other groups have focused on what method government should use to curtail undocumented immigration; these groups therefore might come down on either side of the issue based on agreement or disagreement with the method rather than the goal itself.

Then, too, in the decade-long immigration debate that culminated in the passage of IRCA, new players stepped to the forefront who vigorously pursued civil rights issues even for undocumented aliens. African Americans, Hispanics, and the ACLU were the new sentinels who would scan the legislative environment for residues of old or new racial and ethnic discrimination.

The "problem" of undocumented immigration has been fostered within a distinctly American phenomenon which has been referred to as "front door–back door" adjustments to existing immigration policy, that is, using legal and not so legal means to rework immigration policy to fit vested interests of specific groups.

Immigration policies have never been based on clarity regarding what types of people should come to America, under what circumstances, and with what effects for the rest of the country. Instead, policy has been produced incrementally, out of carefully crafted compromises among many conflicting interest groups. It is often the intended and unintended effects of a specific immigration policy that, in a sense, "causes" the next needed change in immigration policy. Apropos to this study, to a great extent, the unintended effect of intensifying the volume of Third World legal immigration created by the 1965 immigration law had paved the way for the enactment of IRCA in 1986. In turn, IRCA ended up paving the way for the 1990 and 1996 immigration laws.

While patterns of ethnic prejudice and racial discrimination in immigration policy are historically irrefutable and stand unto themselves, organized labor had often been effective in "piggy backing" on these sentiments to curtail the flow of immigrants based on labor's belief that new immigrants threaten the domestic workforce. Capital and agribusiness interests have also been ingenious at creating alternative routes, often outside of official immigration policy, to provide what they feel is a needed stream of low-skilled foreign workers.

Finally, the decade-long immigration debate of the mid-1970s and 1980s had been fueled by the same factors as past immigration policy; that is, issues of ethnicity and race and the interests of labor and capital. However, as we shall see in Chapter 4, the uniqueness of the immigration debate that culminated in the passage of IRCA rested on its almost exclusive focus on curtailing undocumented immigration and the new alignments and realignments of the various interest groups on either side of the questions of legalization, employer sanctions, and the "need" for foreign workers.

Chapter 4

The Legislative History of IRCA: Key Provisions

Governments can err, Presidents do make mistakes, but the immortal Dante
tells us that divine justice weights the sins of the cold-blooded and the
sins of the warm-blooded on different scales. Better the occasional faults
of a government that lives in a spirit of charity than the consistent omis-
sions of a government frozen in the ice of its own indifference.

Franklin Delano Roosevelt

Passage of the legalization and employer sanctions provisions of IRCA, the
heart of the reform package, grew out of a basic political decision to change
immigration policy in order to prevent future undocumented immigration into
the United States (North and Portes 1988, p. 1). The law was specifically
designed to curb undocumented immigration in two fundamental ways: (1)
by erecting barriers through the use of employer sanctions which would, in
effect, turn off the job magnet that draws the undocumented to U.S. borders,
and (2) by offering an amnesty program and eventual citizenship to the undocumented already in the United States as a prerequisite for good enforcement in the future (Portes and Kincaid 1985, p. 73).

  Although the goals were seemingly straightforward, in reality the centerpiece provisions of IRCA became law only after nearly ten years of congres-

sional debate. Its legislative history, as Fuchs notes, has proved to be "a classic example of pluralistic democratic pressure groups at work" (1990, p. 253).

The following legislative history will try to illuminate the often tortuous path that the legislation took over the years prior to enactment, what compromises were made by which stakeholders, and with what results for policy. The aim of the analysis is to explain why the legalization provision appears to have veered off course during implementation and thus fostered the continued presence of a large residual pool of undocumented immigrants that had become all the more dispossessed as a result of the passage of IRCA. The intent of the analysis is to show that the IRCA legislation was essentially a restrictive package which utilized the employer sanctions provision as the new tool for controlling the influx of new undocumented immigrants, just as prior policies had used "excluded categories," "literacy tests," and "quota systems" to control the flow of legal immigrants (LeMay 1987, p. xiv).

On the other side of the legislative argument, Western growers and secondary market employers, among others, could not be expected to accept penalties on employers for hiring undocumented workers without the quid pro quo of guarantees of other "routes" to temporary foreign workers. Civil libertarians and Mexican Americans in turn would need a generous legalization program if they were to accept tightened sanctions on employers who hire the undocumented (Midgley 1983, p. 65). The tensions between these two central and opposing vantage points indicative of the nation's ambivalence toward immigrants dominated the debate on immigration reform through the 97th, 98th, and 99th congressional hearings.

Although the historical issues of ethnicity and race, and capital and labor relations continued to inform and divide congressional debate on immigration reform, a deepening social consciousness was allowing some interest groups to scrutinize legislative provisions for vestiges of old or new forms of discrimination and racism and to stand opposed.

In the end, however, the compromises that allowed this legislation to finally become law were crafted within a pluralistic political system among so many stakeholders and viewpoints that the process itself may have condemned the final enactment of IRCA to serious implementation difficulties.

THE RECOMMENDATIONS OF THE SELECT COMMISSION: THE ORIGINAL INTENT OF IRCA

Rather than presenting each of the bills that preceded the enactment of IRCA (that is, the SCIRP Commission, the Simpson–Mazzoli and Simpson–Rodino bills in detail), this legislative history, in keeping with the goal of the book, will focus on the major provisions of legalization and employer sanctions, and in an ancillary way, the temporary worker provision.

Beginning in 1971, Congressman Peter Rodino, then chairperson of the House Immigration Subcommittee, held a four-year series of hearings around the country on undocumented Mexicans in the workplace. He became convinced that "the illegal alien displaces American workers, depresses wages, (and) burdens the welfare rolls" (Midgley 1983, p. 52). In 1972 and 1973, Rodino introduced legislation that would penalize employers for hiring undocumented immigrants. Each year the bill "passed the House but failed in the Senate where agri-business interests" held sway (Cockroft 1986, p. 214). In late 1970, the Carter administration put forward an immigration bill initiated by Rodino that contained provisions for both a legalization program and an employer sanctions provision. However, forces opposed to immigration reform and those in favor both quickly scuttled the new bill (LeMay 1987, p. 136).

In 1975, North and Houston presented a research project in which they "set forth the implications for the society at large of toleration of a vulnerable underclass" as a focal point that heightened concern that undocumented immigration adversely affects the pay and working conditions of low-skilled U.S. workers (Midgley 1983, p. 53). The study, though never published, made its way through the corridors of power in Congress, as Midgley points out, "through the good offices of the Secretary of Labor" (1983, p. 53). In spite of the fact that the overall findings of the study were that "undocumented immigrants impose few strains on the nation's social service network and overall infrastructure," a critical attitude toward illegal immigration had been set (Papademetriou and Di Marzio 1986, p. 34).

Five interagency task forces emanating from the executive branch were set up during the 1970s to deal with immigration matters (LeMay 1987, p. 136). In 1978, the Select Commission on Immigration and Refugee Policy, headed by Reverend Theodore Hesburgh, former head of the Civil Rights Commission, and Dr. Laurence Fuchs, the noted political scientist from Brandeis University, were invited, by then, by President Carter and the Congress to address the problem of undocumented immigration and to propose solutions. SCIRP's findings, as noted earlier, are widely regarded as the authoritative source of the original intent of the Immigration Reform and Control Act of 1986 (Midgley 1983, p. 54).

The bill creating the Select Commission noted "the paucity of hard data . . . on the impact of immigration, both legal and illegal," and also called upon SCIRP to "assess the social, economic, political and demographic impact of previous refugee programs" (Midgley 1983, p. 54). In May 1979, SCIRP held its opening meeting in the Capitol. Public members appointed by President Carter were Theodore Hesburgh, then president of Notre Dame; Rose Matsui Ochi, executive assistant of the mayor of Los Angeles; Joaquin Francisco Otero, vice president of the Brotherhood of Railway and Airline Clerks; and Judge Crus Reynoso, associate justice, California Court of Appeals. Cabinet members included Benjamin Civiletti, attorney general; Patricia R. Harris, secretary of health and human services; F. Ray Marshall, secretary of labor; and Ed Muskie, secretary of state. Appointed by the president of the Senate were Dennis DeConcini (D-Arizona), Edward M. Kennedy (D-Massachusetts),

Charles McMatthias, Jr. (R-Maryland), and Alan K. Simpson (R-Wyoming). The speaker of the House of Representatives appointed the following members: Hamilton Fisk (R-New York), Elizabeth Holtzman (D-New York), Robert McClory (R-Illinois), and Peter W. Rodino, (D-New Jersey) (Hesburgh, Final Report 1981, p. vii).

A shift in the Senate majority in 1981 from the democrats to the republicans meant that an important shift in the Select Commission occurred as well. Senator Edward Kennedy, the commission's leading immigration expansionist was replaced by the leading restrictionist, Republican Senator Alan Simpson (Midgley 1983, p. 58).

Reverend Theodore Hesburgh, chairperson of the Commission, and Dr. Laurence Fuchs, executive director of the commission's staff, played a considerable role in formulating the questions and recommendations that came from the Select Commission. Both, according to Midgley, shared "an affectionate regard for the immigration of the past hundred years and were inclined to refer to the benefits of immigration, when the opportunity arose" (1983, p. 55).

SCIRP recommended a slight increase in legal immigration, enforcement measures to deter illegal immigration specifically through employer sanctions, an amnesty or legalization program for most undocumented aliens already in the country, and revisions in the existing temporary worker program, called H-2 workers, to help agricultural growers who would stand to lose their large undocumented immigrant labor force if employer sanctions were adopted. The Select Commission was, in effect, recommending the "closing of the back door to undocumented immigration while opening slightly the front door to accommodate more legal immigration" (LeMay 1987, p. 136). The commission held that:

[It] is not the time for large-scale expansion in legal immigration—for resident aliens or temporary workers—because the first order of priority is bringing undocumented/ illegal immigration under control while setting up a rational system for legal immigration. (Hesburgh, Final Report 1981, p. 8)

A more cautious approach was recommended, "to bring the benefits of immigration to the United States without exacerbating fears—not always rational—of competition with immigrants" (Hesburgh, Final Report 1981, p. 9). Of specific significance for this study is the explanation of Hesburgh in the final report regarding the legalization recommendation:

The Commission has not chosen a very early cutoff date (such as the 1970 date incorporated in the Carter Administration's 1977 proposal), because it would permit the participation of too few undocumented/illegal aliens, leaving the United States with a substantial, underclass still in illegal status. (Hesburgh, Final Report 1981, p. 77)

Hesburgh described the commission's reasoning in the following way: "The strong desire to regain control over United States Immigration Policy is one of several reasons for the Commission's unanimous vote to legalize a substantial portion of the undocumented/illegal aliens now in our country" (1981, p. 12). And, in harkening back to America's historic immigration policies, Hesburgh made the case for the commission's choice of a substantial legalization program:

Another [reason] is its acknowledgement that, in a sense, our society has participated in the creation of the problem. Many undocumented/illegal migrants were induced to come to the United States by offers or work from United States employers who recruited and hired them under protection of present United States law. A significant minority of undocumented/illegal aliens have been part of a chain of family migrants to the United States for at least two generations. After entering for temporary work, these migrants began coming to the United States before this nation imposed a ceiling on legal immigration from the Western Hemisphere in 1968 and a 20,000 per country visa ceiling on legal immigration for each Western Hemisphere country in 1976. (Hesburgh, Final Report 1981, pp. 12–13)

Hesburgh indicated that the commission, "in setting a cutoff date of January 1, 1980, had selected a date that will be near enough to the enactment legislation to ensure that a substantial portion of the undocumented/illegal population would be eligible." The commission concluded that the numbers of persons eligible for the legalization program would vary in relation to the residency or cutoff date that was chosen. SCIRP's staff estimated that if the cutoff date was set at *two* years, "approximately *60 percent* of the undocumented population in the United States would qualify for legalization. . . . If the cutoff date were increased to *three* years, an estimated *45 percent* of those with undocumented status" would qualify (Hesburgh, Final Report 1981, pp. 77–78, emphasis added). Presumably, a cutoff date of nearly five years (which the Congress ultimately adopted) would yield eligibility for approximately 15 to 30 percent of undocumented immigrants already in the country.

Without knowing if and when the Congress might act on their recommendations, the commission did not recommend a specific number of years to the Congress. Hesburgh points out that many of the commissioners supported the idea "that Congress choose a period of time that balances the desire for incorporating a substantial number of undocumented/illegal aliens into the United States with the necessity of limiting participation to those who have established some equity in this country" (Hesburgh, Final Report 1981, p. 78). However, Hesburgh himself disagreed with the commission's decision not to vote for a specific cutoff date:

I believe that the Commission made a mistake in not specifying a period of residence for undocumented/illegal aliens who would qualify for the legalization program. . . . My own preference is for the law to state that aliens must have resided in this country continuously for a period of one year prior to January 1, 1981. Under this stipulation, the law would require a period of no less than two years of continuous residence, if the legalization program begins in January 1982, and three years if it begins in 1983. (Hesburgh, Final Report 1981, pp. 337, 338)

Hesburgh makes a point that is key to the argument set forth in this book: namely, the effect of having an early cutoff date on the undocumented population (the one finally adopted by IRCA was nearly five years):

Any longer period of continuing residence (than two to three years) would run the risk of defeating the purposes of the legalization program as recommended by the Commission and present the United States with the serious problem of continuing a substantial underclass with its negative effect on United States society. It would also complicate our enforcement efforts in curtailing new illegal migrations and visa abuse. *If the period is as long as three years, I believe that the residual group should not be kept in an underclass status.* (Hesburgh, Final Report 1981, p. 338, emphasis added)

That the commission intended the legalization program to be generous in granting amnesty to most undocumented immigrants is clear from their own choice of words: "Many of the Commission majority . . . hold the view that Congress should act as quickly as possible to establish a legalization program that will include the majority of undocumented/illegal aliens currently in this country" (Hesburgh, Final Report 1981, p. 84).

In reaching its conclusions, the commission stated its view that

The existence of a large undocumented/illegal migrant population should not be tolerated. The cost to society of permitting a large group of persons to live in illegal second-class status are enormous. Society is harmed every time an undocumented alien is afraid to testify as a witness in a legal proceeding (which occurs even when he/she is the victim), to report an illness that may constitute a public health hazard or disclose a violation of United States labor laws. (Hesburgh, Final Report 1981, p. 7)

Laurence Fuchs, commenting on the legalization recommendation of the commission indicates that:

Legalization was seen by all sixteen Commissioners as part of the overall enforcement strategy and as a way to improve the health of American democracy. (In Glazer 1985, p. 32)

In this sense, it is clear that in the foundational work of SCIRP, the commission did not set out to place the legalization provision in opposition to or in a quid pro quo position to employer sanctions. In an article written in 1985, Fuchs speaks to this issue:

The companion recommendation of employer sanctions, the legalization of a substantial number of illegal aliens already in the country—was not recommended by the Select Commission as a trade-off to employer sanctions, as was frequently stated during the Congressional debate on Simpson–Mazzoli, but because the existence of such a large underclass is harmful for several reasons. It is a invitation to further illegality, since illegal aliens are often afraid to report crimes committed against them. It invites the breaking of the laws regulating wages and work standards. (In Glazer 1985, p. 32)

In this same text, Fuchs clearly states the commission's underlying posture: "In fact, the commission's recommendations were pro-immigration and anti-illegal immigration, fundamental positions with which I agree" (in Glazer 1985, p. 18). Fuchs then clarifies what he means. Being anti-illegal immigration meant being for the rule of law:

To the Select Commission it (the rule of law) meant essentially two things, that the United States should not permit the buildup of an underclass society living outside the protection of the law; and that measures to enforce the immigration law should be effective without themselves engendering lawlessness or promoting an abridgement of due process. (In Glazer 1985, pp. 21–22)

Each version of IRCA, whether the Simpson–Mazzoli bill or the Simpson–Rodino bill that reached the floor of the House and Senate, followed in broad outline the substantive work of the Select Commission on Immigration and Refugee Policy. It remains to be seen in this analysis how the cutoff date for legalization in the final draft of IRCA was set at nearly five years—a considerable departure from the intent of the commission. Then, too, there was the gradual separation of the twin provisions of employer sanctions and legalization into two opposing postures toward immigration rather than two consistent strategies working together to reduce future undocumented immigration, as the commission had intended.

THE 1981 OMNIBUS BILL: THE SIMPSON–MAZZOLI BILL

A task force on immigration and refugee issues was set up by President Reagan in March 1981 to review the SCIRP proposals. The results of the administration's thinking were contained in the bill known as the Omnibus Immigration and Control Act of 1981. While the elements in Reagan's bill were taken up again by Simpson and Mazzoli, Reagan's bill was never acted upon by Congress.

The six elements in the omnibus bill were as follows: (1) An amnesty or legalization provision which offered resident alien status after a ten-year waiting period; citizenship could be applied for at the ten-year point as well. (2) A guest worker provision which would provide for fifty thousand Mexican workers to enter the United States each year, and gradually increasing to hundreds of thousands annually. (3) Employer sanctions on employers of more than four undocumented immigrants who "knowingly hire" them. Fines up to a thousand dollars per instance would be imposed on the employer. (4) A boat people provision that would intercept Haitians heading for the United States and create detention camps to hold them prior to their deportation hearings. (5) Strengthening of enforcement through a 50-percent increase in the INS budget and the addition of 1,500 border patrol officers. (6) Limits on legal immigration through admitting 610,000 new immigrants yearly. Preference would be shown to Mexican and Canadian entrants (LeMay 1987, p. 138).

In his boat people provision, Reagan was responding to public opinion regarding the unwelcome influx of Haitian and Cuban boat refugees. Midgley notes that Reagan's employer sanctions provision shows the reluctance of his administration to adopt this measure, evident by "the exemption of small employers from the penalties and the rejection of any new means of substantiating worker identification." So the legalization provision was also watered down to a form "of inferior status" for the undocumented for a considerably longer period of time (ten years) than the amnesty program envisioned in the SCIRP recommendations (1983, p. 64).

The entirely new element in the Reagan proposal was the temporary worker provision. Midgley noted that Reagan had to assure "a ready supply of labor" to his southwestern supporters. "Their price for the stricter enforcement and tighter control of immigration was the temporary foreign worker program that the President had included in his 1981 proposal." However, unemployment during this time was high and forecasted to continue. Given this circumstance, "the President could not be sure that Congress would enact a temporary worker program." During a period of high unemployment, the argument could not be used with much confidence that there were many available jobs that U.S. citizen workers would not accept. Similarly, legalization of unauthorized workers would be less palatable during difficult economic times. Midgley noted that "civil libertarians and Mexican-Americans could not be expected to accept penalties on employers of unsanctioned workers without the quid pro quo of legalization" (1983, p. 65). Briggs indicated that, for a variety of reasons, the Reagan bill "was so deficient in its content that it was never acted upon by Congress" (1987, p. 1004).

In its place, a bipartisan bill was proposed in 1982 by Senator Alan Simpson (R-Wyoming) and Congressman Romano Mazzoli (D-Kentucky). Their bill, the Immigration Reform and Control Act of 1982, known as the Simpson–Mazzoli bill, was a comprehensive proposal directed toward reform of all aspects of the nation's immigration system. Cockroft asserts that supporters of the bill made it appear to be "patriotic, restrictionist, and in the interest of labor."

The bill was presented as a means of regaining control of the nation's borders, of slamming the door on unwanted Mexican "wetbacks," of stemming a potential tidal wave of Caribbean and Central American "boat people" and "feet people," and of preserving the nation's culture (1983, p. 218)

An underlying nativism was apparent in the wording used by Senator Alan Simpson (R-Wyoming) in presenting his legislative proposal:

If language and cultural separatism rise above a certain level, the unity and political stability of the nation will, in time, be seriously eroded. A common language and a core public culture of certain shared values, beliefs, and customs makes us distinctly "American." (Cockcroft 1983, p. 222)

Midgley points out that in keeping with his "colorful western colloquialisms," Simpson often used the metaphor of a three-legged stool "to symbolize the elements of immigration reform that he regarded as primary: enforcement of the law at the borders and, internally, penalties on employers who persistently employed unsanctioned immigrants, and better worker identification" (1983, p. 66). Absent from the "stool" analogy was any word on amnesty as a means of "wiping the slate clean" as a prerequisite to better enforcement as had been recommended by the SCIRP report.

To ears tuned for echoes of historic strains of ethnic and racial antagonism, Simpson's public remarks could be viewed as a source of renewed discomfort:

My concern [is] that we exercise caution in the number of immigrants, especially those whose cultural background may seem more different or more foreign to the bulk of our people than have past immigrants seemed to the majority population at those times. (in Midgley 1983, p. 66)

All other immigration proposals that the Congress grappled with up to 1986 were variations on the Simpson–Mazzoli bill of 1982. It formed the foundation for all other proposals entertained by Congress. Along the way it had many near-death experiences, in Congress in 1982, only to be resuscitated in 1983, revised in both chambers of Congress in 1984, presented again in 1985, where it nearly died, then was finally passed in October 1986.

The major provisions of the 1982 Simpson–Mazzoli bill were

The Legalization Provision. The Senate version provided temporary resident status to undocumented immigrants who could prove that they had been in the United States since 1980, and permanent resident status to those undocumented aliens who could prove that they had been in the United States since January 1, 1977. The House version also offered permanent resident status to all undocumented aliens who could prove that they had been in the United States since January 1, 1977 and offered permanent resident status to all undocumented aliens who have lived in the United States since January 1, 1982.

Employer Sanctions. The House and the Senate version differed somewhat, but provided for civil and criminal penalties for employers who "knowingly" hire undocumented aliens. The first offense would result in civil penalties; repeat offenders were subject to criminal fines of up to $3,000 per offense and up to one year in prison. Neither version called for a national identity card, but it did suggest the development of a "tamper proof" method of verifying a worker's authorization to work. The Simpson–Mazzoli bill did not contain a new temporary worker program, but it did agree with the commission's recommendation by proposing ways to make the H-2 program more available to employers (Briggs 1987, p. 1004). The expanded and streamlined Simpson–Mazzoli H-2 proposal was intended to make it easier for employers to import temporary and other workers from Mexico and thus ease the loss of undocumented aliens (Crewdson 1983, p. 319).

OPPOSITION TO EMPLOYER SANCTIONS AND THE LEGALIZATION PROGRAM

Opposition to one or other of the bill's provisions began to develop almost immediately among various interest groups. Briggs points out that the employer sanctions provision "was strongly supported by the AFL-CIO and by such influential business groups as the National Association of Manufacturers, the Business Roundtable, and the National Federation of Independent Business" (1984, p. 171).

On the other hand, the strongest opposition to employer sanctions came "from Hispanic organizations and from other groups that had traditionally expressed concern for the plight of illegal immigrants" (Briggs 1984, p. 171). These groups feared that employers would use employer sanctions as an excuse to discriminate against persons who were "Spanish looking" or Spanish speaking.

The U.S. Commission on Human Rights, voicing the sentiments of other civil liberties organizations, voted 3 to 2 against the concept of employer sanctions.

An employer sanction law would be an unjustifiable imposition of law enforcement duties upon private persons and corporations with undesirable consequences not only for the employer, but for due process of job applications. Moreover, increased employment discrimination against United States citizens and legal residents who are racially and culturally identifiable with major immigrant groups could be an unintended result of an employer sanctions law. (U.S. Commission on Civil Rights 1980, p. 74)

The National Association for the Advancement of Colored People endorsed penalties for employers of undocumented immigrants as a way of protecting American workers. However, African American congressmen vigorously opposed employer sanctions. Their decision was based on "their desire for solidarity with their Hispanic colleagues," the heavy presence of Hispanics in many of their districts, their innate caution regarding any provision that "smacked of discrimination," and the presence and growth of a West Indian influence in the African American community (Simcox 1988, p. 6).

The Mexican/American Legal Defense and Education Fund made their case thus:

For Americans who share the physical characteristics of persons thought to be undocumented, employer sanctions will exacerbate . . . discrimination. Well-meaning employers . . . will shy away from hiring us. Racist employers will simply use the fear of sanctions as an excuse to avoid hiring us. (Cose 1992, p. 151)

Senator Edward Kennedy offered amendments to delete provisions from the Simpson–Mazzoli bill which were of most concern to Hispanic Americans, easing family reunification, eliminating the H-2 temporary worker expansion program and introducing a "sunset" provision which would have eliminated the employer sanctions provision in three years if a pattern of discrimination against foreign-looking and foreign-speaking American citizens could be established. Crewdson reports that "concerns for humanitarian and civil liberties were running counter to the reformist sentiments in the Senate. All of Kennedy's proposals were defeated" (Crewdson 1983, pp. 323,324).

Alan Cranston pointed out, however, that employer sanctions would, in effect, require all American citizens to establish "their legal right to work"— an idea that was "offensive and repugnant to the concept of individual dignity and liberty" (Crewdson 1983, pp. 323, 324).

Jesse Helms (R-North Carolina), the congressional "standard bearer of the Moral Majority," spoke of "being offended by the very notion" of the legalization program.

It is wrong to reward law breakers, to set in motion a program which will encourage further law breaking and which will polarize our society. Citizenship in our great Republic is too precious to grant in a vast blanket program to millions of foreign nationals who have flagrantly violated our law. (Crewdson 1983, pp. 324, 325)

Although Helm's amendment to kill the legalization program entirely was defeated 82 to 17, it paved the way for tightening the conditions under which amnesty would be available.

In defending the amnesty provision, Simpson attempted to interject some realism into the debate by pointing out to the Senate that because "they [the undocumented] could not be located when they were coming in, how can we find them to get them out?" (Crewdson 1983, p. 324). Simpson, in countering Helms, spelled out the central purpose of the legalization program in clear, insightful terms:

Legalization is not a reward for violation of our immigration laws. It is a very practical solution to a very serious national problem. We have a fearful subculture of human beings in the United States, who, according to the information received at hearings in the subcommittees, for fear of being discovered, fail to report crimes against their property, their person, or their family, do not seek medical help unless it is to give birth to a U.S. citizen, and who will not complain about exploitation in the workplace. That cannot be good for this country and somehow, indeed, it diminishes us in known and unknown ways. (In Gimpel and Edwards 1999, p. 156)

Congressional debate on the legalization and employer sanctions provisions was taking place at the same time that millions of American citizens were out of work. Crewdson points to the fact that some congressmen began talking about passing the Simpson bill without any amnesty program whatsoever and began referring to it as a "jobs bill," an idea that was "politically difficult to resist" (1983, p. 331). It was in this unstable political climate that the bill proceeded haltingly through the halls of power.

The 1982 bill that the Senate finally passed provided for a generous, expanded temporary worker program that at the same time "would have greatly restricted the role of the Department of Labor in the certification process." By way of contrast, the original Simpson–Mazzoli bill would have changed "the Department of Labor certification from its current advisory status to a mandatory requirement" (LeMay 1987, p. 141).

The employer sanctions provision of the 1982 bill proposed to exclude any undocumented immigrants already employed before the bill was enacted. They would be "grandfathered" into their present employment. It also required the administration to work toward the development of a tamper-proof ID card within three years (Le May 1987, p. 141). Penalties for violating employer sanctions would also be more severe than in the original Reagan version.

The bill passed in the House in 1983, but "died" in the Senate, "weighed down" by nearly three hundred amendments. In 1984, the bill was resurrected and passed in both houses but with different versions. The House version responded to "pressures from growers of perishable crops" with a vastly expanded temporary worker program which, LeMay notes, was "reminiscent of the bracero program begun during World War II." Leon Panetta (D-California), the amendment's sponsor, argued that "the imported workers program would not allow their exploitation because of its provision that their wage and working conditions could not 'adversely affect' those of domestic workers" and that the temporary workers "were free to leave the growers who brought them in." The new program would have allowed for "as many as .5 million workers annually." Jim Wright, then House majority leader, added an amendment requiring a two-year waiting period as a legal resident before applying for permanent residency. Added to this was the proviso that they "be employable," study English, and enroll their children in school. In the election year of 1984, Congress failed to find an alternative version of the two bills, in large part because of democratic opposition (1987, pp. 141, 142).

In assessing the employer sanctions and amnesty provisions of the Simpson–Mazzoli bill, Cornelius P. Mantoya noted that:

The authors of the pending legislation, Senator Simpson and Congressman Mazzoli, have at least practiced the virtue of candor. They have described their bill as a "leap into the dark," but stand by the proposal because, they allege, previous employer sanction laws have failed to reduce the hiring of illegal immigrants due to a lack of proper enforcement. They argue that with enough money, personnel, and a strong will to enforce, employer penalties can be an effective means of immigration control. Unfortunately, there is not a shred of evidence to support this claim. (in LeMay 1987, p. 142)

By May 1985, Simpson once more introduced another version of his bill, minus his cosponsor Mazzoli, who distanced himself from the bill due to lack of support for it from the Hispanic caucus and the democratic leadership. While the centerpiece provisions of employer sanctions and legalization remained the same, some of the details began to change. Gone was the requirement that employers validate employee documents. Inserted into the bill was a tamper-proof social security card and steep penalties for counterfeiters (LeMay 1987, p. 142).

The amnesty or legalization provision was substantially weakened. The 1984 bill had called for the legalization program to begin ninety days after the bill was passed; the 1985 bill called for a presidential commission to first certify that the new law had "substantially" reduced the undocumented population—a daunting if not impossible phenomenon to document. The cutoff date for amnesty in this version was January 1, 1980, which would mean at least a five-year cutoff point depending on the enactment date. The process of legalization was projected to take a year to accomplish. The bill also placed a $1.8-billion limit on federal reimbursements to states for services related to the legalization program. Although congressional critics questioned this financial limit, Simpson was intent on passage of the bill through carefully crafted compromises (LeMay 1987, p. 142). However, any bill with any hope of passage had to address the issue of providing western growers with an adequate supply of agricultural workers and, at the same time, do so in a manner that reduced their exploitability (Simcox 1988, p. 8).

In July 1985 Rodino and Mazzoli offered yet another version of the bill. This time the employer sanctions provision had stiff legal penalties for employers "who knowingly hire illegal aliens," and the amnesty provision was updated to 1982. Because of concerns about discrimination from the Hispanic caucus, the bill contained a provision for the Justice Department to set up a special council to investigate allegations of civil rights violations (LeMay 1987, p. 143).

The House Judiciary Committee wanted the amnesty provision to be linked to employer sanctions. The administration's support for an amnesty provision was weakened by various interest groups, particularly "business interests in the border states" who strongly opposed legalization. Clearly, the question of how many undocumented immigrants "should" be legalized and at what expense to the taxpayer was an issue. The Reagan administration wanted to avoid any major federal expenditures. Thus, as Portes and Kincaid report, "tortuous negotiations focused on the size of the amnestied population (to be determined by a cut-off date of arrival in the U.S.) and the divisions of responsibilities between the federal and local governments for accommodating the amnesty population" (1985, p. 74).

In 1985, the Senate and Judiciary Committee scuttled attempts made by Senate democrats to fashion the Senate version more in the likeness of the House version. Again in 1985, Simpson introduced his bill to the Senate, but six House committee members continued to tinker with it. In particular, the Judiciary Committee was deadlocked over the temporary farm worker provision (LeMay 1987, p. 143, 144). The most formidable political opponent, however, came from western and southwestern growers whose business relied on undocumented immigrant workers. Their posture was that if government wanted to block undocumented immigration, it would also have to turn on the "spigot" of a temporary foreign worker program of some kind. Ultimately, as Fuchs maintains, these "employers wanted to be in a position to turn on and off the spigot to regulate the flow of workers from Mexico" (Fuchs 1990, p. 253).

When the bill seemed destined to die once again because of continued haggling, Charles Shumer (D-New York) along with Congressmen Berman and Panetta began to craft a plan "to reconcile these conflicting interests" (Simcox 1988, p. 8).

THE SHUMER COMPROMISE

When the bill hit the floor of the Senate in September of 1986, no other aspect of the new proposed law engendered more discord than the issue of temporary foreign workers. As Fuchs points out, "In the end, the growers were able to persuade Congress to enact a special agricultural worker program; but this time they were obliged to accept one fundamentally different from the bracero programs that preceded it" (Fuchs 1990, p. 253). Simcox points out that "any bill seeking to capture the support of both the western growers and the Farm Workers Union, which carried the AFL-CIO's proxy on farm labor issues, would have to provide for an adequate supply of agricultural workers and at the same time reduce their exploitability" (Simcox 1988, p. 8).

Shumer's plan stated that "the Attorney General could grant lawful permanent resident status to any illegal immigrant who could prove that he had been working in perishable agriculture for at least 20 full days from May 1, 1985 to May 1, 1986" (Briggs 1987, p. 1009). The final version stated ninety full days. With passage of IRCA, this amnesty program would become known as the SAWs program or Seasonal Agricultural Workers, as distinct from the LAWs provision which is the subject of the research in this book. The LAWs provision refers to the Legalization of Authorized Workers.

With the Shumer amendment, agricultural workers who had been granted legalization would be free to work where they chose, even outside of agriculture, and would be able to become either resident aliens or eventually citizens if they chose. In this proposed legislation, Congress was explicitly rejecting the idea of a subclass of undocumented or guest foreign workers who would be condemned to an "inferior status because they were aliens" (Fuchs 1990, p. 253).

Under Shumer's amendment, if foreign farm workers quit work, the plan allowed for replenishment of the labor force through additional undocumented immigrants who could in turn become resident aliens with the option of citizenship (Briggs 1987, p. 1009). With passage of IRCA this provision became known as the RAWs, or Replenishment of Agricultural Workers provision.

Clearly, employer sanctions would have deprived southwestern agribusiness of "several hundreds of thousands" of their current undocumented immigrants. The Shumer proposal addressed this issue, and by allowing these farm workers to be legalized, the plan "overcame the fears of supporters of immigration reform who were opposed to any kind of guest worker program." The farm workers, under the Shumer amendment, could enjoy many of the protections afforded nonagricultural citizen workers such as joining a union or leaving farm work for better opportunities. Briggs refered to Shumer's plan as "this ingenious compromise" that balanced the interests of such diverse groups as the growers, unions, and the Hispanic lobby. The other stroke of genius was the new rule of debate which forbade "any amendment to be made to the fragile terms of the Shumer Amendment." The employer sanctions and the legalization provisions could be debated, but not the Shumer Amendment on foreign agricultural workers: "Its fate was linked to passage of the overall bill" (1987, pp. 1010, 1011).

With the Shumer amendment in place, momentum began to build. Interest groups that were firmly opposed to the bill began to break rank. Five members of the Hispanic caucus voted in favor of the bill which was a significant shift that justified movement by other interest groups (Simcox 1988, p. 9).

The attitude of rank-and-file Hispanic Americans came into play as well. These constituents believed that the status quo was hurting their job opportunities and urged "their representative to vote for immigration reform." A number of African American congressmen switched their vote to endorse the bill, believing that their constituents were concerned about the negative impact of undocumented immigration in terms of job competition (Simcox 1988, pp. 9–10).

LeMay suggests that during 1985 and 1986, "Congress was in a better mood to pass some sort of an immigration law than in previous years" because of the deterioration of the Mexican economy and the record number of undocumented Mexican aliens caught by the INS, representing a rise of 31 percent in apprehension, an increase of approximately 1.8 million persons. For liberal opponents of the reform bill, the growing conservative mood of the country did not bode well for further resistance. They feared "even stricter legislation in 1987" (1987, p. 144).

For Simcox, passage of IRCA confirmed the idea that undocumented immigration was no longer simply a problem for border states or agribusiness interests, but had become in the public mind "a problem affecting every corner of the nation" (1988, p. 10). In the end, the Shumer amendment won "enough of the Hispanic/liberal/union votes in Congress for passage of the bill" (LeMay 1987, p. 145).

According to LeMay there were six holdout issues yet to be resolved. They were as follows:

1. The House bill wanted employer sanctions terminated after six-and-one-half years. Both the administration and the Senate stood opposed.

2. The House bill had the Moakley amendment granting suspension of deportation for undocumented Salvadorans and Nicaraguans. The administration and the State Department stood opposed.

3. Barney Frank (D-Massachusetts) had proposed a nondiscrimination provision which the Senate and the administration strongly objected to.

4. The two versions proposed different cutoff dates for the legalization provision. The House version had a cutoff date of January 1, 1982 while the Senate version had a cutoff date of January 1, 1980.

5. On reimbursements from the federal government, the House version wanted 100-percent federal reimbursement while the Senate version proposed a $3 billion figure to be dispensed over the six years following implementation.

6. Howard Berman (D-California) added a provision for free legal counsel for farm workers admitted under the H-2 temporary work program (1987, p. 145).

LeMay goes on to describe how a 1986 conference committee settled on a series of compromises to resolve these six issues. The House agreed on no automatic end to employment sanctions. In exchange, the Senate agreed to a three-year review, and a "sunset provision" that said that if employer sanctions showed a pattern of discrimination against foreign looking or foreign speaking authorized workers, the provision would be repealed. The House gave up the Moakley provision. The Senate agreed on antidiscriminatory provisions proposed by Barney Frank (D-Massachusetts) and free legal counsel for H-2 workers. Resolution of the funding issue came when both House and Senate agreed on $1 billion each year for a period of four years. The unspent portion would be rolled over into the next year through to fiscal year 1994. The amount of federal payments for supplemental Social Security income and Medicaid was to be deducted from the $1 billion appropriation. Finally, the Senate agreed to the House's "more liberal" version of the amnesty program's cutoff date of January 1, 1982 (LeMay 1987, pp. 145, 146).

Under the circumstances these compromises represented the best that they could do. The qualifier, "under these circumstances," answers the question of why Congress decided on the conservative five-year cutoff date. At the time, it appeared "liberal" and was indeed the best that could be done. In the words of Mazzoli, "It's not a perfect bill, but it's the least imperfect bill we will ever have before us" (LeMay 1987, p. 146). *Time* summarized its impression of the "drawn out, convoluted and acrimonious" legislative journey of IRCA in the following way:

Seldom has so important an issue come so far so often in the legislative process with those concerned with it having so little idea of its potential effects. No one can say for sure whether immigration reform can be made to work, what it might cost and, most important, whether it would ultimately help or hurt the country. In that information vacuum, politicians, businessmen, labor leaders, minority representatives and social scientists have taken positions on all sides of the issue. (LeMay 1987, p. 146)

LeMay, somewhat prophetically, summarized his view of the legislative history of IRCA thus:

Certainly the review of the history of immigration policy enables one to predict one thing with a fair degree of certainty: that this major revision, as have all those enacted in the past, will surely have some unforeseen consequence that will create new problems and will sow the seeds for the next revision. (1987, p. 147)

The research examined in the next chapter focuses on one such "unforeseen consequence" at the local level of implementation. Legislators anxious to see the reform package finally passed into law did not anticipate the many problems in the legalization program's design which created difficulties that prevented a large percentage of the undocumented population from being legalized. Nor did they visualize what the effect might be on this "left behind pool" of undocumented persons when confronted with full implementation of employer sanctions. The research in Chapter 5 focuses on the lives of specific groups of undocumented immigrants at the local level where policy decisions intersect with the real lives of individuals in ways that even the architects of the 1986 immigration law may not have intended. In the end, the legalization and employer sanctions provisions were vastly different from the original intent of the Select Commission. The commission made clear in its report that it had not chosen "a very early cutoff date because it would permit the participation of too few undocumented/illegal aliens, leaving the United States with a substantial underclass still in illegal status" (Hesburgh, Final Report 1981, p. 77). As the commission members indicated in their report, a cutoff date of five years would yield eligibility for approximately 15 to 30 percent of the undocumented immigrants already in the country.

A central premise in this book has been that the legalization and employer sanctions provisions of IRCA embodied in the same piece of legislation contradictory attitudes toward undocumented immigrants. We have seen in the journey through the legislative process how two strategies that were intended to work in harmony to prevent future illegal immigration ended up as bargaining chips that whittled away at the original intent of the commission. Mayhew points out that "it is difficult to state with any degree of certainty what the 'intended' goals of Congress are for any particular piece of legislation" (1974, p. 47). A new law such as IRCA passes through debate, compromises in subcommittees, discussions on the floors of both Houses and in full view of the administration, public interest groups, lobbyists, and constituents over years of deliberation, in IRCA's case nearly ten years. Often such legislation ends up as a series of carefully crafted compromises geared toward "passage." In this sense, the "intent" of a particular piece of legislation or programmatic detail concerning implementation does not drive the process; instead it is driven by compromise itself.

Just as the 1965 immigration law backfired in its attempts to eliminate discrimination in immigration law and ended up exacerbating it, so too the 1986 law which was intended to "wipe the slate clean" of undocumented immigrants resulted in driving them further into a nether world by depriving them of the right to work. Its failure to control undocumented immigration into the United States in a sense spawned the more mean-spirited 1996 immigration law in a political climate that had grown increasingly hostile to new arrivals unsanctioned by law. As stated earlier, IRCA's failure to stem undocumented immigration can be seen in an INS update published in the *New York Times* on February 8, 1997, announcing that "Illegal Immigrants Rose to 5 Million in 1996" (Schmitt 1996, p. 9). These approximations mirror pre-IRCA estimates of the subterranean shadow population living in the United States despite Congress's promises to the contrary.

STUDIES ON THE TWO MAIN PROVISIONS OF IRCA: LEGALIZATION AND EMPLOYER SANCTIONS

The legalization or amnesty program began on May 5, 1987 and continued for one year. Thus far no known empirical research has been done on the social and economic effects of the legalization program on undocumented individuals or groups aside from the research that informs this book. However, four studies focused on midpoint (Heilberger 1987), third quarter (Meissner 1988), interim (North and Portes 1988), and endpoint evaluations (LeMay 1994) of the effectiveness of the legalization program in terms of the response level of undocumented immigrants to the amnesty program. They also examined some of the specific problems that emerged during the implementation phase.

Studies on the Implementation of the Legalization

The first study, conducted by the Massachusetts Immigration and Refugee Advocacy Group (MIRA), provides a framework in which to consider some of the specific barriers to successful implementation of the legalization program from the perspective of the immigrant-serving community and its clients, undocumented immigrants. Although the report carries some ideological burden in terms of its positive stance toward the undocumented, the barriers to effective implementation that the report identifies have also surfaced in each of the three other studies on the legalization program.

Keeping the Promise? A report on the Legalization Program of IRCA in Massachusetts at the Halfway Mark reports that six months into the legalization program, 4,204 undocumented immigrants had applied for legalization in Massachusetts as compared to INS's projections of 60,000 eligible persons

(1987, p. 1). The authors, Heilberger, Adieli, and Fried, identify five specific barriers to the effective implementation of the amnesty provision. The report notes that many of the problems that arose in the implementation phase would not have occurred if the law had contained a more current eligibility date rather than a cutoff date of nearly five years. The second barrier to legalization identified in the study was the family unity issue. IRCA called for applicants to be individually eligible for legalization, irrespective of the status of other family members. It was silent on the question of relatives of undocumented aliens who were themselves ineligible. Because migration generally occurs in stages, split eligibility within families emerged as a central issue. However, the report notes that INS regulations did not deal specifically with the problems of ineligible family members. "Because applicants must report the names of their ineligible family members on legalization applications, many have not come forward out of fear of exposing their family members to detection and possible deportation" (Heilberger, Adieli, and Fried 1987, p. 6). A family fairness policy was adopted to try to rectify the situation, although it was introduced very late into the implementation process.

A third deterrent to legalization was the requirement that applicants demonstrate they had been living and working in the United States since before January 1982. Proof such as rental receipts and verification of employment were required. The report suggests that the "target population, almost by definition," had sought for the sake of survival "to avoid the creation of such paper trails." The study indicates that "many employers, landlords, and former associates refuse to supply documentation to legalization applicants in the mistaken notion that they are exposing themselves to civil and criminal penalties for violations of labor tax laws" (Heilberger, Adieli, and Fried 1987, p. 10).

A fourth deterrent was the delays and problems in mounting a public education campaign that resulted in a "fatally slow" start for the $10.7 million, INS-sponsored public education effort. "Time and again, experts from the twelve countries that had conducted legalization programs emphasized that a massive public education effort [was] the key to the success of such programs" (Heilberger, Adieli, and Fried 1987, p. 10).

The fifth barrier pointed out in this study was fear of the INS. The authors note how difficult it was for the INS to mount a one-year campaign to convince undocumented immigrants that it was safe for them to come out of the shadows to seek and achieve legal status in this country. For years this same population lived in fear that the INS would apprehend and deport them. The general pattern six months into the program was that those with simpler cases came forward first while "others with more complex cases are hanging back." The tragedy was that "as the clock ticks away, many must still be persuaded that they will experience no negative consequences from the INS as a result of seeking legalization." Acknowledging the fear factor, an agent from the Springfield, Massachusetts legalization office stated, "They don't trust us. I suppose there's some reason for that." On the other hand, an agent from the

Boston office claimed, "We're trying to highlight that there is no reason for fear. We're here. We're ready. We're extending ourselves to anyone." In the meantime, the undocumented were using up precious time as "the only true test of the safety of the program" (Heilberger, Adieli, and Fried 1987, p. 12).

A second study, *The Legalization Countdown: A Third Quarter Assessment*, authored by former INS Commissioner Doris Meissner and Demetrius Papademetriou, examined issues around the central objective of the legalization program: "that all eligible undocumented aliens be given a reasonable chance of obtaining legal immigration status" (1988, p. vii). The assessment was based on extensive interviews of INS personnel, immigrant-serving agency staff, and immigration advocacy groups in the seven states and major metropolitan areas which accounted for the overwhelming majority of applications.

The study's findings point to "the formal, contracted, public information effort" as seriously inadequate and lacking "an outreach effort" that would "pierce" barriers to the undocumented population. The study points out that the final mid-January publicity campaign was based on greater clarity on the public relations needs and was a promising development. This effort had two major objectives: (1) to "create the impetus to apply because time is running out"; and (2) to "supply accurate information about who can apply." However, the lack of a national information strategy that would include both the media and outreach and the absence of a "collaborative public–private effort have contributed to large nationality and regional variations" in terms of response to the legalization program (Meissner and Papademetriou 1988, pp. viii, ix).

The report also points to the lack of outreach activity to groups and institutions that the immigrant community has historically trusted, such as churches, community organizations, schools, unions, employers, and ethnic leaders. Regulatory policies are also pinpointed as barriers to eligibility. In particular, although the INS had "made important adjustments, modifications and clarifications" to the guidelines, these "changes had not been effectively communicated." The family unity issue is also alluded to as a deterrent to applying for legalization on the part of some of the undocumented. The report notes that "Congress should have addressed the family unity question" in the legislation phase. As it was, the INS appeared vulnerable to charges of insensitivity to families and thus this issue was a "weak link" in the reimaging of the INS (Meissner and Papademetriou 1988, pp. x, xi). Lack of clarity on documentation requirements had also hindered the legalization process.

The report summarized its conclusions by noting that "the documentation requirements, ineligibility of family members and distant cutoff date pose severe constraints. Even if an additional 300,000 to 400,000 applicants could be reached, the size of the remaining illegal population in the country would be almost twice the number who would have been legalized. Congress' stated objective of mandating legalization to enhance future immigration enforcement cannot be achieved through the program it enacted" (Meissner and Papademetriou 1988, pp. xviii, xix).

The study pointed out the existence of pervasive tensions between the immigrant serving community and the INS in interpreting the intent of Congress, to be generous or not so generous in granting legal status to aliens.

The major finding in this study was that the legalization program required "immediate, firm policy intervention so that a unique opportunity for legalization" of the large residual population "will not be squandered" ((Meissner and Papademetriou 1988, p. vii). According to the study, excessive documentation requirements, the eligibility of family members issue, and the conservative cutoff date posed severe restraints on applicants. Based on these constraints, the authors conclude that even if there were a last minute surge of applicants, the size of the remaining illegal population would be almost twice the number who would have been legalized.

A third study, *Through the Maze: An Interim Report on the Alien Legalization Program* by David North and Anne Marie Portes, studied (1) the differential impact of the law in different segments of the undocumented alien population; and (2) the number of aliens who have applied for legalization. The methodology used in this study consisted of interviews with INS staff and immigrant-serving staff in ten different states along with six surveys of eligible aliens in four cities. (The study also examined the SAWs program which is not the subject of this book.)

The conclusions of this study are that the legalization program has had more skewed effects than had been predicted. In particular, the law has been more beneficial to Mexican nationals than to other aliens, more beneficial to men than to women, and more beneficial to aliens in the southwest than to aliens in the northeast. "Many eligibles appear to have "self-selected out" of the program for a variety of reasons, among them "fear of misinformation" (North and Portes 1988, p. 71).

Although the study points out there is but one law (IRCA) and one set of regulations, there is also a great deal of decentralization in the legalization program. What might account for some of the differential effects is the fact that the 107 local offices of INS have some free rein in interpreting regulations and in mounting public education campaigns.

In this study the authors used the Census Bureau benchmark figures for the number of undocumented illegal aliens who might be eligible for amnesty. With adjustments for undercounts of minorities and single males, their estimated figure as of April 1980 was that at least 2.5 million persons (out of the estimated 3.9 million illegal aliens thought to reside in the United States) would be eligible for legalization. At the point of the study when the report was being written, 1.2 million persons had applied. The authors suggest that the shortfall in applications is accounted for by the nature of the endeavor. Their basic theme throughout the report was that the legalization program was a growing and changing organism. Through time, INS had eased some of its procedures and had, albeit "late in the game," increased its public education program. They concluded that "a substantial number of eligible, potential applicants, however, have not yet applied for the program, and many of these will probably not do so between now and May 4, 1988" (North and Portes 1988, p. 71). The recommendation of this study was a six-month extension of the deadline to November 30, 1988, so that INS could reach out to non-Mexican populations and to eligible immigrants who may have self-selected out of the program. INS would have time to clear up areas of controversy with the immigrant-serving community and could mount a national, broad-based, public education program that actually reached the undocumented community.

Although limited in scope, each of these studies points to a legalization program that was seriously off course in relation to its major objective of "wiping the slate clean" of the large, residual pool of illegal aliens residing within the United States.

Two of the major barriers, the eligibility date and the family unity issue were not fully addressed by Congress. As is evident from the legislative history, the eligibility date, which was not updated as congressional debate continued through nearly ten years, fell victim to the political process itself. So, too, the family unity issue may hinge on the fact that United States law always deals in terms of the individual. Skeptics, however, point to these two central issues as indicative of a legalization program that Congress never intended to be generous and inclusive. The other barriers, which rested on INS interpretation, have met the same fate; critics point to rigidity in interpretation of policies as a sign of exclusion and repression.

Michael LeMay in his 1994 book, *Anatomy of a Public Policy: The Reform of Contemporary American Immigration Law*, examined the implementation of IRCA's legalization provisions, the LAWs, SAWs, and RAWs programs. In particular, LeMay notes that the INS had only "six months to plan, design and implement the LAWs program," the one that is at issue in this book (p. 83). He offers a "tentative evaluation of IRCA" and notes some of the ups and downs of the implementation process from the perspective of the INS.

Responses from qualified designated entities (QDEs), separate offices set up by the INS to process legalization applications, noted in particular "the tremendous difficulty involved in securing the proper documents." Other barriers included the long delay in setting up the QDE offices and the confusion and inaccuracies in interpreting the rules and regulations. The responses also pointed to complaints that INS staff were "subjective," "rude," "racist," and "insensitive" to clients. In one-third of the responses, INS agents were described as having "bad attitudes" and "misinformation" (LeMay 1994, pp. 89, 90). The size and complexity of implementing IRCA's legalization program was extremely taxing on the INS along with the "360-degree" angle change in their mission from enforcement and apprehension to coaxing the undocumented to step forward. The family unity issue was noted by many of the respondents as a major deterrent, although interpretations varied widely across different jurisdictions.

The cost of the legalization process that was borne by the applicants was also reported to be a disincentive. Because the program was largely "self-funded," the undocumented were charged an application fee of $185 for each applicant with a family cap of $420. When costs associated with medical exams, fingerprinting, photographs, and possible legal fees were added to the application fee, the process itself was thought to be cost prohibitive for many applicants. The conservative cutoff date of nearly five years was also seen as "deleterious to the success of the legalization program" (LeMay 1994, p. 92).

LeMay states that "the specific date chosen by Congress created a new class of people who would likely remain in an underground illegal status—the very condition that the law intended to avoid. Moreover, the INS program of family fairness unfortunately did little to assuage these problems" (1994, p. 92).

Other barriers to legalization included confusion about "excluded categories" such as misdemeanors, felons, and interpretations of regulations regarding "likely to become a public charge," "continued residency," and "continuous physical presence."

Studies on the Implementation of the Employer Sanctions Provisions

The employer sanctions provision of IRCA was designed to stem the availability of jobs for undocumented immigrants, thus removing what Congress saw as the primary magnet for those entering the United States illegally. The law's most important points have been summarized by Stone in the following manner:

1. Employers must not "hire, recruit, or hire for a fee" anyone who is not authorized to work in the United States.

2. Employers must verify the work authorization of every employee hired after November 6, 1986 by requiring them to show documents or combinations of documentation specified by the INS on its I-9 form. As long as a "good faith effort" has been made to inspect a worker's documents, employers are not legally responsible for hiring someone whose documents are fraudulent.

3. Employees on the payroll as of November 6, 1986, no matter what their immigration status, are "grandfathered" in, and the employer may legally continue to employ them without examining documents.

4. Penalties for violating the employer sanctions provision may include fines of up to $3,000 for each unauthorized worker hired and a possible six-month jail term for habitual offenders. Employers who fail to check workers' documentation or file I-9 forms may be fined up to $1,000 per violation.

5. Anticipating that fear of sanctions would cause some employers to avoid hiring anyone who they think may be foreign, Congress added a strong antidiscrimination provision to IRCA. Practices prohibited under the antidiscrimination clause include firing or refusing to hire someone because he or she "looks foreign" or has an accent (1989, pp. 13–14).

The first study conducted by the United States General Accounting Office (GAO), entitled *Immigration Reform: Employer Sanctions and the Question of Discrimination*, was published in March 1990. The GAO was mandated by the Immigration Reform and Control Act of 1986 (IRCA) to issue three annual reports to Congress for the purpose of determining whether IRCA's employer sanctions provision had (1) created unnecessary burdens on employers, (2) been carried out satisfactorily, and (3) resulted in a pattern of discrimination against eligible workers. IRCA provided Congress with a "sunset" provision: an option to repeal the employer sanctions provision if the GAO determined in its third report "that a widespread pattern of discrimination has resulted against eligible workers seeking employment" solely from the implementation of this law. For this third report, GAO (1) reviewed federal agency implementation of IRCA, (2) reviewed discrimination complaints filed with federal agencies and data from groups representing aliens, and (3) used additional methods to obtain data on IRCA's effects. These methodologies included a statistically valid survey of over 9,400 of the nation's employers, which projects to a universe of about 4.6 million employers (Browsher 1990, p. 3).

In collaboration with the Urban Institute, GAO did a "hiring audit" in which pairs of persons matched closely on job qualifications applied for jobs with 360 employers in two cities. One member of each pair was a "foreign-appearing, foreign-sounding" Hispanic and the other was an Anglo with no accent.

The GAO results found that the employer sanctions law had apparently reduced undocumented immigration and was not an unnecessary burden on employers, that it had generally been carried out satisfactorily by INS and the Labor Department, and that it had not been used "as a means to launch frivolous complaints against employers" (Browsher 1990, p. 3). They also found that "a widespread pattern of discrimination" against immigrants based on their "national origin" had resulted from the implementation of employer sanctions.

The question they had to resolve in their study was, given the fact that GAO found "widespread discrimination," could they link it to the implementation of employer sanctions? GAO's response was a resounding "yes." Based on the responses of employers to key questions GAO asked about their hiring behavior and how it related to the provisions of IRCA, GAO concluded that a substantial amount of discrimination did occur as a result of IRCA. An estimated 461,000 employers or 10 percent of all those surveyed reported national origins discrimination as a result of the law. However, the other 90 percent did not. Thus GAO concluded that discrimination was serious but not pervasive. GAO saw three options open to Congress: (1) leave IRCA as it is for the present, (2) repeal the employer sanctions provision, or (3) amend IRCA's verification of employment provision to reduce the law's discriminatory effects (Browsher 1990, p. 4). Clearly Congress chose option one and left the employer sanctions provision as originally written. No further action has been taken although public demonstrations in the year 2000, which the AFL-CIO joined, demanded repeal of employer sanctions as well as the development of a new legalization program for the undocumented.

A second study, a state agency task force then appointed by Governor Cuomo of New York and chaired by Cesar Perales, commissioner of the Department of Social Services, was formed to gauge the effects of the new immigration law on New York residents and government agencies. Their report, entitled *The Immigration Reform and Control Act of 1986: New York's Response*, was published in March 1987. The methodology used in this study was a questionnaire designed to survey state agencies responsible for serving the undocumented immigrant population and implementing the provisions of the new law. The task force report documented discrimination arising from the implementation of the employer sanctions provision.

In one month the task force documented sixty cases of discrimination based on IRCA. Several factors were reported to have fostered acts of discrimination under the new law: the delay in issuance of federal regulations interpreting IRCA, employer discrimination or ignorance of the provisions of IRCA, and failure of the Justice Department to appoint a special council to deal with these problems (Perales 1987, p. 5).

The report states,

Much confusion surrounds the system of sanctions attached to hiring undocumented aliens. Most of the reported firing of undocumented aliens have occurred because employers have not understood that undocumented workers hired before November 6, 1986 may continue to work without risk of the imposition of sanctions. As regulations are not yet final, employers also are unclear on the types of records they will be required to maintain. Employees who do not fully understand the provisions of the new law are unable to protect themselves against unlawful or unnecessary firing or firing practices. (Perales 1987, p. 5)

The most widespread problem reported in New York was the firing of undocumented workers who were hired prior to November 6, 1986. The report described one such individual, "Manuel A.," as a fictional example of the effects of the new immigration law on the lives of undocumented immigrants residing in the country. Manuel's story was reported in a survey conducted by the task force committee.

Manuel immigrated to New York from Peru a number of years ago. Since 1984, he has supported himself, his wife, and his children by working steadily at the Fictitious Maintenance Company of Long Island. In December, panicked by news reports of the new immigration law, yet having received no details from the federal government, Manuel's employer demanded an original work permit document from him. In February, when Manuel could produce only a copy of this document, he was fired. The employer later said he "only wanted to hire American workers."

The report goes on to state some facts about Manuel's case:

1. Manuel should not have been fired. Any undocumented immigrant hired before November 6, 1986, does not have to be fired. Rather they are "grandfathered" into their present job.

2. The "Fictitious Maintenance Company" would not have been subject to any sanctions at the time it fired Manuel. Employers were not penalized for hiring undocumented workers until after an initial educational period that ended in June 1987.

3. After being fired, Manuel could not then legally get another job in order to support his family. After November 6, 1986 employers could not "knowingly" hire undocumented immigrants who were not authorized to work.

4. Manuel lost his job and therefore his employment record which was needed to prove "gainful employment," and so he had lost his chance to become a citizen. Now unemployed, Manuel was not eligible for unemployment insurance, Medicaid, or AFDC benefits. If he sought state public assistance to support his family, Manuel would be showing himself to be "in danger of becoming a public charge" and therefore he would lose his eligibility to become a citizen.

5. Finally, the report states that "Manuel has no redress before the law" (Perales 1987, pp. 5, 6, 7).

Other accounts of discrimination cited in the report included authorized alien workers being threatened with firings, Hispanic workers being told to produce "green cards" or be fired, Puerto Rican native-born U.S. citizens being threatened to either produce "green cards" or be fired, and refusals to hire on the basis of national origins. The report states that "the magnitude of such abuse cases appeared to be in the thousands" (Perales 1987, pp. 5, 6, 7).

The results of these two studies suggest that despite the appearance at least the overall goal of employer sanctions had stemmed the tide of undocumented immigration into the United States, a byproduct of the law had been that there was a clear pattern of discrimination against foreign-looking and foreign-speaking authorized workers and violations of the rights of "grandfathered" undocumented workers under IRCA.

Chapter 5 will add to the body of research on the implementation of IRCA through its unique focus on the endpoint of the legislative process: IRCA's impact on specific groups of undocumented Haitian, Irish, and Salvadoran immigrants living under full implementation of employer sanctions. Several of the preceding studies on the legalization and employer sanction provisions of IRCA were helpful in pinpointing specific conditions in the circumstances of the undocumented in the aftermath of full implementation of IRCA and were therefore useful in designing the research that informs Chapter 5.

Chapter 5

The Impact of IRCA on Undocumented Immigrants: A Furtive Exercise in Survival

The indifference of society and of policy makers to the plight of illegal immigrants is one of the most reprehensible aspects of contemporary American life.

V. Briggs

When social scientists design a research project, they are attempting to take a snapshot, a still life frozen in time, of the phenomenon under study. Through the empirical research that informs this book, the curtain is lifted for a time on the little known subterranean world of the undocumented just at the point when the full impact of the legalization and employment sanctions provisions of IRCA could be experienced by specific groups of undocumented immigrants. To suit the purpose of the study, subjects had to be immigrants who remained undocumented even after the legalization program was completed and who were then living under full implementation of the employer sanctions provision. As noted in Chapter 4, less than one-third of the estimated number of undocumented immigrants, or 1,655,676 undocumented immigrants, were legalized through the amnesty program (LeMay 1994, p. 83).

The research project focused on undocumented immigrants from the greater Boston, Massachusetts area who remained trapped within the United States as a result of IRCA, that is, those who came after 1982 and up to 1987 and therefore could not apply for legalization, and in some instances those who came before 1982 but who did not or could not apply for legalization. Obviously, they remained in the United States despite the new law. The research itself gives insights into why they made this seemingly inexplicable decision to remain in the United States despite the hardships. Reasons why they were not eligible for legalization have to do with the barriers written into the legalization program discussed earlier: namely, the conservative cutoff date of nearly five years, the unresolved family unity issue, the high financial cost of applying for legalization, the need for a paper trail to provide documentation (even though it is by not creating a paper trail that they managed to remain undetected), and the lack of a broad-based education effort by the INS to acquaint the undocumented with the amnesty program. Undocumented immigrants were drawn from three ethnic and racial groups: Haitians, Irish, and Salvadorans. The choice of these three groups allowed the researcher to measure the impact of IRCA on black, Hispanic, and white immigrants and to pinpoint whether race or ethnicity played a role in the effects of the legislation on these three groups. These ethnic groups also represented the largest proportion of undocumented in the geographic area. A comparison group from among the three ethnic and racial groups of immigrants who had been accepted for legalization were also needed to function as a control group. The use of control groups allows the researcher to study the experience of two groups who are similar to each other in every respect except one: in this case, immigration status. Thus, when there are significant differences in the responses of the two groups it can be inferred, once the research design has met certain empirical safeguards, that the variable "immigration status" is creating the difference, if differences are found. Even then there are stringent statistical rules governing whether a degree of difference noted between the two groups is indeed statistically significant.

The goal of this research was to see how the twin provisions of legalization and employer sanctions were affecting undocumented immigrants in three areas: their social and economic needs, their utilization of social services, and the responsiveness of the social service system to their needs. There were three assumptions underlying the research. First, immigration status for undocumented immigrants under the 1986 immigration law should be associated with increased social and economic need. Related to this was the second assumption that undocumented immigration status would be associated with a reduction of utilization in social services despite increased need. Third, there would be a reduction in the responsiveness of the social service delivery system to the needs of the undocumented.

Information was gathered through the use of a questionnaire administered within an interview format. Great care was taken to ensure that vulnerable undocumented immigrants were not placed at greater risk of detection as a result of this research project. Prior relationships existed between the researcher and the three agencies used in the study. Under the limitations posed by the difficulty of "finding" undocumented immigrants and their need for anonymity, a random sample was impossible to achieve. In order to produce a random sample, the statistical universe of the undocumented would need to be known which, by definition, is impossible. The criteria used in selecting undocumented and newly legalized immigrants were male or female "heads of households" between the ages of eighteen and fifty-five from Haiti, El Salvador, and Ireland. The willingness of the undocumented to place themselves at risk for this research has provided the ongoing motivation for telling their story.

The total number who participated in the study was ninety immigrants, equally divided between undocumented and legalized. There were thirty immigrants from each of the three racial and ethnic groups:

Ethnic Groups	Legal Status	Number
Haitian immigrants	Undocumented	15
Irish immigrants	Undocumented	15
Salvadoran immigrants	Undocumented	15
Haitian immigrants	Legalized	15
Irish immigrants	Legalized	15
Salvadoran immigrants	Legalized	15
Total		90

The first step in the interview strategy was to meet with the administrators of the three immigrant serving agencies that were targeted to be used in the study because of their services to either Haitians, Irish, or Salvadoran undocumented clients. The purpose of the interview was to explain the research project, elicit agency approval for using a sample of the undocumented and newly legalized clients in the study if the clients agreed, and to review with them confidentiality, the strategy for gaining informed consent from the undocumented and assurance of agency anonymity. This pledge of anonymity was necessary because the IRCA legislation mandated the elimination of federally funded social services to undocumented immigrants. Most of the agencies were scrambling to find creative ways to continue to serve this increasingly desperate group without jeopardizing their federal funding stream.

A second step included securing the approval of the administrators to use one or several of their staff, either social workers or ESL teachers, to conduct the structured interviews of the undocumented and newly legalized immigrant clients. This approach was deemed necessary because of issues of trust, confidentiality, language, culture, and the particular vulnerabilities of undocumented persons before the law. The strategy was to ask the social workers and/or teachers from within each agency to approach clients with whom they had a trusting relationship to ascertain their willingness to be interviewed. As a prelude to this process, the researcher set up training sessions on the purpose of the research, the sampling criteria, how the interviewers were to approach the undocumented and legalized immigrants to ascertain their willingness to be participants in the study, and to acquaint them with the informed consent procedure in which the immigrant would be asked simply to sign with an "x" or any other variation if they agreed to participate. The second part of the training session was devoted to a discussion of the structured interview process and precautions needed to insure reliability in the interview phase. Because the interviews were to be conducted in three languages and by several different interviewers, particular attention was paid to the idea of uniform protocols and neutrality in conducting each individual structured interview.

The training session stressed the importance of seeking precise data and maintaining a neutral stance. Time was devoted to a discussion of the pitfalls of overinterpreting a question or of the interviewer giving the respondent "hints" as to the "right" response through body language and mannerisms.

Next the interviewers were given the questionnaire in their own language and were asked to role play as if they were one of the respondents in order to surface questions and concerns about the instrument and how to handle specific problems that might arise. For example, some felt that the undocumented would not want to reveal their income or other sensitive answers. In this instance, it was pointed out that in the informed consent document, the undocumented had the right to refuse to answer any question or even to leave the interview.

Taking a "snapshot" of these two groups meant creating a questionnaire with a number of scales in which the respondent's answer could be given a numerical weight. In looking at social and economic need, scales were developed in the following areas: depression, stress, health, drug–alcohol use, marital and family relations, housing, financial well-being, and workplace abuse. Added to this were scales that measured utilization of social services by the undocumented and their perception of the responsiveness of the social service system to their needs. Nonparametric statistical tests were then run on the numerical data to determine whether there were statistically significant differences between the two groups on their social and economic need, their utilization of social services, and the responsiveness of the social service system to their needs. Each of the individual scales such as depression, health, or financial well-being could also be tested statistically to see if there were significant differences across the two groups of undocumented and legalized immigrants and between the three racial and ethnic groups.

OVERALL CHARACTERISTICS OF UNDOCUMENTED AND LEGAL IMMIGRANTS

It is noteworthy that gender differences between the undocumented and the legalized immigrants were slight (see Figure 5.1) until compared across the three groups by country of origin (see Figure 5.2). Haitian immigrants were predominantly female (76.7% to 23.3% male), while Irish immigrants

Figure 5.1
Gender: Undocumented and Legalized

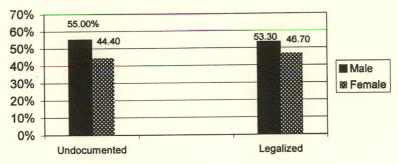

Figure 5.2
Gender by Three Ethnic Groups

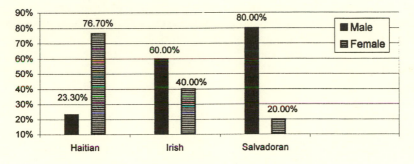

were more heavily male (60% to 40% female). Salvadoran immigrants were predominantly male (80% to 20% female).

While the percentage of "family sharing living space" was higher among undocumented immigrants at 67.4 percent as compared with 45.9 percent for legalized immigrants (see Figure 5.3), the percentage in the Haitian sample is

Figure 5.3
Family Sharing Living Space by Immigration Status

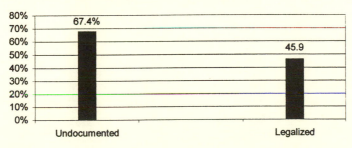

clearly the highest at 71.0 percent, as compared with the Irish at 46.2 and the Salvadoran at 53.8 percent (see Figure 5.4).

When looking at the level of education between undocumented and legalized immigrants, the greatest difference is seen when comparing college education (13.3% for the undocumented as compared with 22.2% for the legalized group; see Figure 5.5). The greatest difference is noted among the Irish when comparing the three ethnic groups. Among the three ethnic groups, 63.3 percent of the Irish finished high school and 30.0 percent finished college, as compared to 6.7 percent of the Haitians completing high school and 10.0 percent completing college (see Figure 5.6).

Present employment showed variation in the percent of undocumented immigrants employed full time: 44.4 percent, as compared with 73.3 percent among the legalized (see Figure 5.7). This is a highly significant finding in the light of the full implementation of employer sanctions which imposes fines and/or imprisonment for employers knowingly hiring the undocumented. Employer sanctions was specifically targeted toward turning off the job spigot that drew the undocumented to the United States. Either employers are ignoring IRCA, or there has been a heyday in cottage industries providing false credentials to the undocumented for a price. Across the three countries, the

Figure 5.4
Family Sharing Living Space by Ethnic Groups

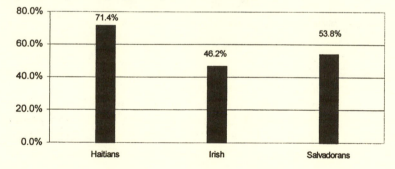

Figure 5.5
Level of College Education by Immigration Status

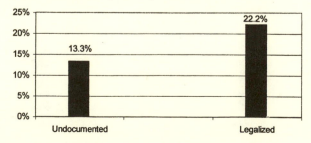

Figure 5.6
Level of Education by Three Ethnic Groups

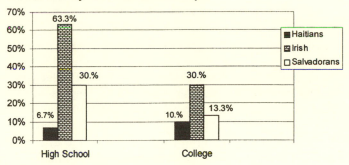

Figure 5.7
Present Employment by Immigration Status

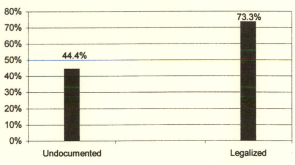

greatest disparity existed between the Irish, 80 percent of whom were employed full time as compared with Haitians, employed at 30 percent full time (see Figure 5.8).

In the "kind of job" category, the percentage of undocumented immigrants working in a "skilled craft" was nearly double the percent of legalized immi-

Figure 5.8
Present Employment by Three Ethnic Groups

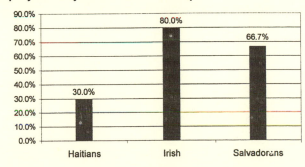

grants at 23.8 percent. The legalized group reported 11.6 percent in the skilled craft category (see Figure 5.9). While the preponderance of "kind of work" was in the service industry for all immigrants, the Haitian figure for the service industry was clearly the highest at 73.1 percent, while the Irish were the lowest at 23.3 percent (see Figure 5.10). In light of educational differences between the two ethnic groups, these results are not surprising.

Under "main reason for coming to America," the differences were slight between the legalized and the undocumented in choosing "political reasons" (see Figure 5.11). However, when compared by ethnicity, the Salvadoran sample was highest in indicating "political reasons" at 43.3 percent, which mirrored the reality of the right-wing war raging in their country at the time. Haitians reported 20 percent, perhaps reflective of the perennial political instability of Haiti. None of the Irish in the study chose this category (see Figure 5.12).

For the undocumented 37.8 percent chose "for a better life" as compared to 33.3 percent for the legalized group (see Figure 5.13). For all three ethnic groups, their highest percentage clustered around "for a better life" (see Figure 5.14).

The mean number of months that the immigrants had been in the United States were fairly similar for both the undocumented and legalized groups.

Figure 5.9
Skilled Work by Immigration Status

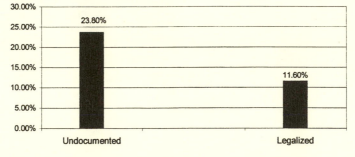

Figure 5.10
Kind of Work–Service Industry by Ethnic Groups

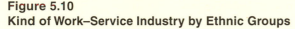
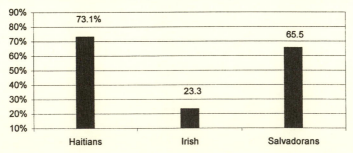

However, Haitians had the highest number of months in the United States, at 109.2 average months, and Salvadorans had the least average number of months in the United States at 51.33 average months (see Figure 5.15). The significance for Haitians was that many of them had been in the country well over the five-year cutoff date for legalization under IRCA and therefore theo-

Figure 5.11
Political Reason by Immigration Status

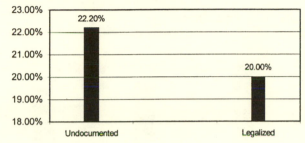

Figure 5.12
Political Reason by Ethnic Groups

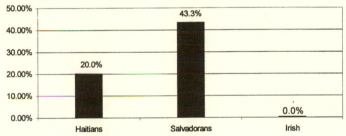

Figure 5.13
"For a Better Life" by Immigration Status

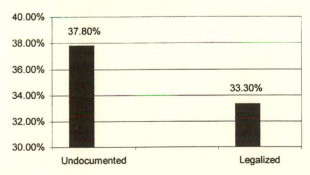

retically could have been legalized if they met the other criteria, possessed the necessary documentation, had sufficient funds, were not worried about the fate of their family, or if they were specifically aware of the program.

In the category "mean hours per week of work" for undocumented ethnic groups, undocumented Haitians had the lowest number of hours per week at 16.36, as compared with undocumented Irish at 37.46 hours and undocumented Salvadorans at 29.73 hours (see Figure 5.16). Of course, theoretically

Figure 5.14
"For a Better Life" by Ethnic Group

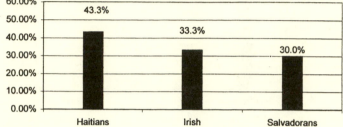

Figure 5.15
Mean Number of Months in United States by Ethnic Group and Immigration Status

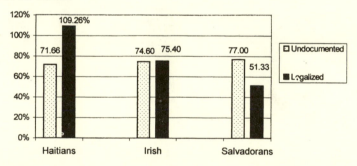

Figure 5.16
Mean Hours of Work for Undocumented Ethnic Groups

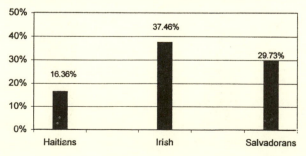

as the result of employer sanctions, the undocumented were not supposed to be working at all at this point. The stipulation that employers "not knowingly" hire the undocumented was beset with loopholes.

"Mean hours per week of work" for the legalized ethnic groups again shows a wide disparity between the Irish legalized group and the Haitian legalized group. Haitians had a 27.50 average hourly workweek while the Irish had a 42.40 average hourly workweek. The Salvadoran legalized immigrants had an average of 34.46 hours of work weekly (see Figure 5.17).

Perhaps the most striking data appears in the last category "mean monthly income" by immigration status (see Figure 5.18). Undocumented immigrants earned an average of $809.97 per month as compared with legalized immigrants at $1,390.97 per month. On one end of the spectrum, Haitian undocumented immigrants earned an average of $382.10 per month while on the other end, Irish undocumented immigrants earned $1,248.90 (see Figure 5.19). Irish legalized immigrants earned more than double ($2,257.14) their Haitian and Salvadoran counterparts. Legalized Salvadorans earned $953.51, and legalized Haitians earned $929.97 (see Figure 5.20).

Figure 5.17
Mean Hours of Work for Legalized Ethnic Groups

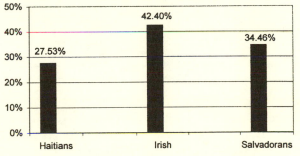

Figure 5.18
Mean Monthly Income by Immigration Status

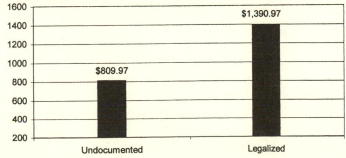

Figure 5.19
Mean Monthly Income by Undocumented Ethnic Groups

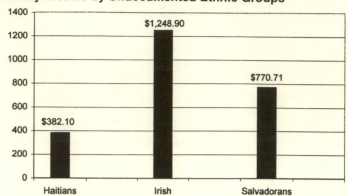

Figure 5.20
Mean Monthly Income by Three Legalized Ethnic Groups

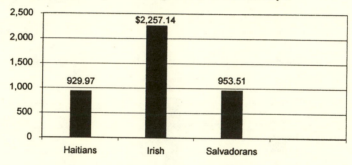

The differences that these descriptive data point to is that beyond immigration status, ethnicity, race, language, and level of education may well have played a significant role in accounting for some of the differences between the legal and undocumented immigrants that we shall discover in this research.

The "snapshot" that these general statistics portray is of an undocumented population that differs from its legalized counterparts on several indicators: level of education, employment, sharing living space, and monthly income. On each of these variables the undocumented are less educated, less employed, share more space with others, and earn decidedly less than the legalized group. When, however, the factor of ethnicity and race enters in, the picture shifts decidedly in favor of the Irish, whether legalized or undocumented, on virtually every variable. The least well-off ethnic group is clearly the Haitians, with 71.0 percent sharing living space, with only 6.7 percent completing high school only, and only 10.0 percent completing college. When looking at "present employment," only 30 percent of the Haitians were employed; those who were working were primarily engaged in the service industry—an over-whelming 73 percent. Not surprising, 43 percent of Haitians came to the United States "for a better life" and had been in the country the longest amount of time and yet seriously lagged behind in numbers of hours of work for both legalized and undocumented Haitians. While the undocumented as a group earned far less than the legalized group, the undocumented Haitians earned a paltry $382 per month in comparison to the Irish undocumented at $1,248. In fact, the legalized Haitians earned less than the undocumented Irish by far—a ratio of $929.97 to $2,257.14.

At this point in the research, specific circumstances in each of the three sending countries are worth mention.

Haiti

For Haitians, the exodus from their home country was in reaction to a steady deterioration in its economic, social, and political situation. Although Haiti was the first black nation in the Western Hemisphere to gain its independence in 1804, it remains to this day the poorest country in the Western Hemisphere. This island nation of approximately six million persons has one of the world's most inequitable distribution of wealth, and under the Duvaliers had one of the worst human rights track records. World Bank figures place illiteracy in Haiti at 80 percent (Johnson 1987, p. 3).

While the Haitian population in the United States includes a number of well-educated professionals, at the time of the research most entrants were "pre-literate in Haitian Creole and had limited education and few transferable job skills" (Seiber 1988, p. 24). Estimates of the size of the population of Haitians in the United States vary widely. INS data and discussions with community leaders place estimates at approximately six-hundred thousand in the early 1980s, with roughly half being undocumented (Foner 1987, p. 200). In the greater Boston, Massachusetts, area where the research took place, the range of Haitians was between thirty and sixty thousand with approximately half undocumented. A large percentage of the Haitian population was composed of young men frequently selected by their families "as most likely to succeed" in the United States, in the sense of being able to help their families in their home country (Seiber 1988, pp. 22, 24). The majority of Haitian undocumented immigrants work at unskilled or semiskilled jobs in factories, the service industry, and domestic services (Foner 1987, p. 136).

Ireland

In the 1980s an estimated 150,000 young Irish men and women left Ireland for the United States without work visas. Theirs had been an economic flight from a stagnant economy and an unemployment rate of 20 percent in the south and up to 60 percent in the north. This economic picture had shifted dramatically in the late 1990s to an Irish economic boom referred to as the "Celtic Tiger" that is unrivaled in Europe. In 1988, net Irish immigration reached forty-five thousand, or as the Boston Pilot reported, "850 a week departing a nation of only 3.5 million persons"—most of them young males— and nearly all poor (Leen 1989, pp. 1, 8). This relatively recent exodus of the Irish to the United States, Australia, and England represented the largest emigration wave since famine times when two million Irish emigrated to the United States between 1845 and 1870.

In the Boston area at the time of the research there were an estimated thirty thousand undocumented Irish who were by and large better educated than prior generations of Irish immigrants. As noted earlier, changes in the 1965 immigration law "were designed to end racial and ethnic discrimination towards non-Europeans" (Leen 1989, p. 1). An unintended consequence of this legislation for the Irish, however, was that visas were nearly impossible to obtain. The twenty-thousand visa limit for each country based on the family preference system favored those who had family members already living in the United States.

In 1986 there were over six hundred thousand legal immigrants admitted to the United States. Of this number, 1,839, or only one-half of 1 percent, were Irish (Leen 1989, p. 8). Likewise, this number had an adverse effect on Irish applications for legalization under IRCA, since their exodus from Ireland had begun after 1983. In 1990 an immigration policy was passed that attempted to rectify this situation for undocumented Irish. Over a three-year period sixteen thousand visas a year, or forty-eight thousand in total, were issued to undocumented Irish either in Ireland or living in the United States with the stipulation that they had an active job offer in the United States. This example is emblematic of the incremental nature of immigration policy in the United States that deals retroactively with snags or unintended effects of prior immigration policy.

El Salvador

By 1988, approximately eight hundred thousand Central Americans resided in the United States, most of whom were undocumented. Of this number, a significant portion were Salvadorans. In the greater Boston area there were an estimated twenty-five thousand Central Americans, with 65 percent of them believed to be Salvadorans and the large majority undocumented (Seiber 1988, p. 14).

The impetus for their exodus in the 1980s from El Salvador, a tiny country of three million persons, was the civil war between ultra right forces and the Marxists. Beyond this, driving factors for emigration were extreme poverty (80% of the Salvadorans lived below the poverty line), and human rights atrocities, in particular the number of "disappeared" and increased right-wing killings. The role of the United States in propping up the militarized right-wing political system to the tune of $3 billion in 1981 was a complicating factor for those fleeing El Salvador. Salvadorans were classified as "economic refugees" rather than "political refugees" and therefore denied entry to the United States.

The 1990 immigration law changed all this by granting asylum for up to two years if the Salvadorans in the United States applied for it. The argument to change their immigration status was that, due to the civil war in El Salvador, undocumented Salvadoran immigrants should be granted asylum if they had "a well founded fear of persecution." Under these terms, Salvadorans could be granted extended voluntary departure status.

In the greater Boston area at the time of the research, over 50 percent of the Salvadorans were single men between eighteen and thirty-five years of age. This age range posed the greatest risk of forced conscription into the army and at the same time the greatest threat for political persecution. Despite all this, Salvadorans remained oriented toward returning home to their country but were aware that peace efforts in their home country remained fragile (Seiber 1988, p. 15).

According to INS Chief of Demographic Statistics Mike Hoefer, as of February 13, 1992, the total number of undocumented immigrants legalized in Massachusetts were 9,859. Nationally, 1,655,676 were accepted for legalization (Lee 1992). In Massachusetts, the INS had originally estimated that there were approximately sixty thousand undocumented persons (Heilberger 1988, p. 4).

THE EXPERIENCE OF BEING UNDOCUMENTED: FINDINGS ON SOCIAL AND ECONOMIC NEEDS

The results of interviews conducted directly with undocumented and newly legalized immigrants are divided into three sections organized around the three assumptions or hypotheses that guided the research; namely that the impact of undocumented immigration status increases social and economic need and at the same time decreases use of social services. Finally, it is assumed that the impact of undocumented immigration on the social service delivery system was to make the system less responsive to the needs of the undocumented.

Two sets of scales were used to test the first hypothesis: that there would be increased social and economic need among undocumented immigrants as compared with their legalized counterparts. To measure social need, five scales were used: a depression scale, a stress scale, a health scale, a marital and family life scale, and a drug and/or alcohol use scale.

Nonparametric statistical tests were run to measure differences between the undocumented group and the legalized group on the five scales and differences among the three ethnic groups as well. As noted earlier, nonparametric means that the sample under study has not been randomly selected[1] and therefore specific statistical tests are utilized. The margin of error used in the study was 0.05 level of significance, meaning that in five times out of one-hundred cases, an error can be made in measuring differences between two samples.

Overall, the results supported the first hypothesis of increased social need. They indicate that there is a statistically significant difference at 0.05 level in the responses of the undocumented on four of the five social needs scales, namely, depression, stress, health, and marital and family relations. The drug and alcohol use scale was the only scale that did not point out a significant difference between the undocumented and the legalized immigrants (see Table 5.1).

When the three countries of birth were compared across the five social need scales, the results pointed to the significance of race and ethnicity as an intervening variable that must be taken into account when considering differences. In four of the five social need scales, the mean score for Haitians showed statistically significant higher levels of need on the depression scale, the stress scale, the health scale, and the marital and family relations scale.[2]

Three scales were used to measure economic need: housing, financial well-being, and workplace abuse (see Table 5.2). The housing scale consisted of eight ordinal level items that measured level of need with regard to overcrowding, heating problems, hot water availability, access to bath, sanitary conditions, experience of homelessness, use of shelters, fear of complaining, and fearfulness of the landlord. A single item, neighborhood safety, asked the participant to rate the degree of safety in his or her neighborhood.

The financial well-being scale consisted of four ordinal level items that measured use of food pantries, financial situation now as compared with be-

Table 5.1
Comparisons of Social Needs Scale by Immigration Status

Social Needs Scale	Mean Rank Undocumented $N = 45$	Mean Rank Legalized $N = 45$	Test Statistic U
Depression $p < .05$, p. 02	51.82	39.18	728.0*
Stress $p < .05$, p .00	53.94	37.06	632.5*
Health $p < .05$, p. 00	53.57	37.43	659.5*
Marital & Family $p < .05$, p. 08 (NS)	50.20	40.80	801.0
Drug / Alcohol Use $p < .05$, p. 05	50.34	40.66	794.5*

Mann–Whitney U Test.

*Represents statistically significant difference.

Table 5.2
Comparison of Social Needs by Country of Origin (higher score equals greater need)

Social Needs Scale	Haiti N = 30		Ireland N = 30		El Salvador N = 30			
	Mean	SD	Mean	SD	Mean	SD	Df	F Ratio
Depression (Subset Haiti) p <.05, p. 00	13.00	2.42	9.06	2.59	10.60	3.49	2	14.227*
Stress (Subset Haiti) p. <.05, p. 00	13.00	2.90	10.46	2.20	11.36	2.25	2	8.433*
Health (Subset Haiti/El Salvador) p <.05, p. 00	5.93	2.11	3.10	2.02	5.30	2.74	2	12.363*
Drug/Alcohol p<.05, p. 186 (NS)	9.33	1.56	8.96	1.47	8.63	1.35	2	1.715
Marital / Family (Subset Haiti/El Salvador) p<.05, p .00	15.90	3.71	6.63	5.52	12.56	4.51	2	30.634*

Analysis of Variance (ANOVA), p < 0.05, p. 00.

*Represents statistically significant difference.

fore coming to the United States, financial situation comparing now with five years ago, and expectation of financial situation five years hence. Four individual questions asked for the primary source of income, amount of income for one month, number of persons relying on this income in the United States, number of persons relying on this income in birth country, and number of benefits (out of a possible five).

The workplace abuse scale consisted of nine ordinal level items that asked the respondent questions with regard to whether they had been paid less than the minimum wage over the last year, had they been asked to work overtime without receiving overtime pay, whether their wages had ever been held back, if they worried about being fired, if they felt, as an immigrant, they had no rights, whether they wanted to join a union but did not, whether they were fearful of being reported to INS, whether they worried that their work environment was unsafe, and whether they felt trapped in a dead-end job.

The results document significant differences between the legalized and the undocumented immigrants on all three scales. Specifically they consistently point to greater need among the undocumented (see Table 5.3). When the

Table 5.3
Comparison of Economic Need Scales by Immigration Status (higher score equals greater need)

Economic Needs Scale	Mean Undocumented N = 45	Mean Legalized N = 45	Test Statistic U
Housing < .05, *p.00	58.61	32.39	422.5*
Financial Well-Being < .05, p.00	52.12	38.88	714.5*
Workplace Abuse < .05, p.00	53.74	34.17	502.5*

Mann–Whitney U Test, p < 0.05, *p. 00.

*Represents statistically significant difference.

three "countries of origin" were examined on the three economic need scales, only one scale, housing, was found to be significantly different across the three countries, Haiti and El Salvador in particular (see Table 5.4).

Since the results were not significant on two of the three economic need scales, the lack of difference among the three groups adds strength to the conviction that legal status, not country of origin, accounts for the differences found in the economic need results. When the results of both the social and

Table 5.4
Comparison of Economic Needs by Country of Birth

Economic Needs Scale	Haiti N = 30 Mean	SD	Ireland N = 30 Mean	SD	El Salvador N = 30 Mean	SD	Df	F Ratio
Housing (Subset Haiti/El Salvador) p < .05, p. 00	14.26	3.43	11.13	2.58	13.90	3.20	2	9.183*
Financial Well-Being p < .05, p. 01 (NS)	3.83	1.46	3.06	1.31	3.46	1.45	2	2.212
Workplace Abuse p < .05, p. 12 (NS)	15.34	5.62	13.46	3.23	13.26	3.06	2	2.179

Analysis of Variance (ANOVA).

*Represents statistically significant difference.

economic need scales were mingled together and compared among undocumented Haitian, Irish, and Salvadorans, the results indicate greatest need among undocumented Haitians and least need among undocumented Irish (see Table 5.5). When all the need scale results were mingled together and compared among legalized Haitians, Irish, and Salvadorans, the results reinforced the same trend found among the undocumented: namely, greatest need among the Haitians and least need among Irish immigrants (see Table 5.6).

The study also examined several social and economic variables (using chi square tests) by comparing the responses of the legalized and undocumented immigrants' experience of homelessness, source of income, and number of work-related benefits that they received. In a comparison of the legalized with the undocumented on the issue of "experience of homelessness," the results showed a statistically significant difference between the two groups, with the undocumented reporting a greater amount of homelessness. The undocumented experienced more homelessness than the legalized group and at a statistically significant level (see Table 5.7). When "experience of homelessness" was compared by country of birth, the findings were again significant in that the Haitians reported more experiences of homelessness than either the Irish or the Salvadorans (see Table 5.8). When "source of income" was

Table 5.5
Need Levels among Undocumented Haitians, Irish, and Salvadorans

Undocumented Haitians N = 15		Undocumented Irish N = 15		Undocumented Salvadorans N = 15			
Mean	SD	Mean	SD	Mean	SD	Df	F Ratio
94.6	16.79	75.93	10.49	87.46	9.68	2	8.21*

Analysis of Variance (ANOVA), p > .05, *p. 00.

Table 5.6
Need Levels among Legalized Haitians, Irish, and Salvadorans

Legalized Haitians N = 15		Legalized Irish N = 15		Legalized Salvadorans N = 15			
Mean	SD	Mean	SD	Mean	SD	Df	F Ratio
85.26	12.78	58.33	8.00	73.26	7.95	2	28.17*

Analysis of Variance, p > .05, *p. 00 (Subset Haiti, El Salvador).

Table 5.7

Comparison of Experience of Homelessness by Immigration Status

Homelessness	Undocumented N = 45		Legalized N = 45	
	Number	Percent	Number	Percent
Never	28	68.3	42	93.3
Sometimes	13	31.7	3	6.7
Total	41	100.0	45	100.0

$\chi^2 = 13.05^*$, p. 00, df = 2.

Table 5.8

Comparison of Experience of Homelessness by Country of Birth

Experience of Homelessness	Haiti N = 30		Ireland N = 30		El Salvador N = 30	
	Number	Percent	Number	Percent	Number	Percent
Never	20	66.7	25	83.3	25	96.2
Sometimes	10	33.3	5	16.7	1	3.8
Total	30	100.0	30	100.0	26	100.0

$\chi^2 = 16.33^*$, p. 00, df = 4.

compared with immigration status, the differences between the undocumented and legalized immigrants were statistically significant. Of the undocumented, 75.6 percent report employment as the main source of income as compared with 88.9 percent in the legalized group (see Table 5.9).

Interestingly, both the undocumented and legalized Irish immigrants reported 100 percent employment as their "source of income" (see Table 5.10). Salvadoran undocumented immigrants reported employment at 80 percent, and the legalized group of Salvadorans reported 86.7 percent employment as their source of income. This outcome, well after implementation of employer sanctions, corroborates the ineffectiveness of employer sanctions as a tool in turning off the job magnet. These findings clearly show that the majority of the undocumented were still working as of 1992, and in the case of Irish undocumented, they were 100 percent employed. Apparently, the lure of a cheap, silent labor force continues to dominate employer choices even after

Table 5.9
Crosstabulations of Source of Income by Immigration Status

	Undocumented N = 45		Legalized N = 45	
Source of Income	Number	Percent	Number	Percent
Employment	34	75.6	40	88.9
Relatives / friends	5	11.1	4	8.9
Public benefits	2	4.4	-	-
Savings	-	-	1	2.2
Other	4	8.9	-	-
Total	45	100.0	45	100.0

Table 5.10
Employment as Source of Income for Three Ethnic Groups

	Number	Percent
Irish		
Undocumented = 30	15	100.0
Legalized = 30	15	100.0
Salvadorans		
Undocumented = 30	12	80.0
Legalized = 30	13	86.7
Haitians		
Undocumented = 30	7	46.7
Legalized = 30	12	80.0

the implementation of employer sanctions with its threat of fines or imprisonment for hiring the undocumented.

Last, the results of cross-tabulations of benefits by immigration status indicate differences in the number of benefits between undocumented immigrants and the newly legalized group. The benefits described in the questionnaire were medical insurance, life insurance, private retirement plan, sick leave, vacation, and maternity leave. Of the undocumented, 75.6 percent report no benefits as compared with 24.4 percent for the legalized group (see Table 5.11).

When the number of benefits was compared by undocumented and legalized Haitian, the results indicate differences between the two groups. Un-

Table 5.11
Crosstabulation of Benefits by Immigration Status

Number of benefits	Undocumented N= 45		Legalized N = 45	
	Number	Percent	Number	Percent
None	34	75.6	11	24.4
1	7	15.0	8	17.8
2	1	2.2	6	13.3
3	3	6.7	4	8.9
4	-	-	13	28.9
5	-	-	3	6.7
Total	45	99.5*	45	100.0

*Indicates a rounding error.

documented Haitians reported 93.3 percent had no benefits as compared with 40.0 percent for legalized Haitians (see Table 5.12). When number of benefits was compared with Irish undocumented and legalized immigrants, the results indicated that 73.3 percent of undocumented Irish had no benefits as compared with 20.0 percent for the legalized group (see Table 5.13). When Salvadoran immigrants were compared by immigration status on the study variable "number of benefits," the results showed that 60.0 percent of undocumented Salvadorans had no benefits as compared with 13.3 percent for the legalized group (see Table 5.14). Overall, the results mean that the undocumented groups report having far less benefits than the legalized groups.

In summary, the individual social and economic need variables reveal significant differences between the undocumented and the legalized sample on several social and economic need variables: homelessness, monthly income, and benefits. Beyond this, the results indicate that country of birth is playing a significant role in accounting for differences between the legalized and undocumented groups on several different variables: homelessness, monthly income, and number of benefits. In turn, the data suggest that differences among the three cultural groups may result from other factors beyond immigration status, such as differences in ethnicity, race, language, and education.

While the results in general support the first hypothesis that the undocumented immigrants will have increased social and economic needs as compared with legalized immigrants, the data also suggests that other intervening

Table 5.12
Crosstabulations of Number of Benefits by Haitian
Undocumented and Legalized Immigrants

	Undocumented N = 15		Legalized N = 15	
Number of benefits	Number	Percent	Number	Percent
0	14	93.3	6	40.0
1	-	-	3	20.0
2	-	-	3	20.0
3	1	6.7	-	-
4	-	-	3	20.0
Total	15	100.0	15	100.0

Table 5.13
Crosstabulations of Number of Benefits by Irish
Undocumented and Legalized Immigrants

	Undocumented N = 15		Legalized N = 15	
Number of benefits (out of possible five)	Number	Percent	Number	Percent
0	11	73.3	3	20.0
1	2	13.3	3	20.0
2	1	6.7	2	13.3
3	1	6.7	1	6.7
4	-	-	3	20.0
5	-	-	3	20.0
Total	15	100.0	15	100.0

variables such as those mentioned earlier are playing a significant role in the differences noted. For example, how much does race and ethnicity factor in? How much does education or the ability of the undocumented white Irish to "pass" as legalized in the larger white and often Irish milieu of the Boston area factor in? These variations point to the differential impact that public social policy can have on some groups. Often it is the poor, the least educated, and those already burdened by language and race differences that are most negatively affected by restrictive social policy measures.

Table 5.14
Crosstabulations of Number of Benefits by Salvadoran Undocumented and Legalized Immigrants

	Undocumented N = 15		Legalized N = 15	
Number of benefits	Number	Percent	Number	Percent
0	9	60.0	2	13.3
1	5	33.3	2	13.3
2	-	-	1	6.7
3	1	6.7	3	20.0
4	-	-	7	46.7
Total	15	100.0	15	100.0

FINDINGS ON UTILIZATION OF SOCIAL SERVICES BY THE UNDOCUMENTED

The second assumption undergirding the research was that undocumented immigrants would use fewer social services after the implementation of IRCA, even though it was assumed that the study findings would show that their social and economic needs had increased. In order to test this assumption, three utilization scales were developed, a "resource utilization scale," a "degree of comfort" in seeking services scale, and a "reluctance factor" scale in approaching help through social services. As we shall see, the results support this hypothesis in the findings of two out of the three scales. The results on the degree of comfort scale indicate that there is a significant difference in the responses of the undocumented as compared with legalized immigrants in terms of their degree of comfort in seeking services. The mean rank score for the undocumented is 37.08, and for the legalized, 53.92, meaning that the legalized groups are more comfortable in seeking services than are the undocumented (see Table 5.15). Likewise, in the third scale, "reluctance factors" related to asking for help through social services, there was a significant difference in the undocumented as compared with the legalized immigrants. The legalized had higher scores indicative of less reluctance in seeking services (see Table 5.15).

The results on the resource utilization scale show that there is not a significant difference in the use of resources between the undocumented and legalized immigrants. However, when the scores of all three scales were combined to form one utilization score, the results were statistically significant in terms of the differences between the undocumented and the newly legalized.

When the three scales were combined to form one "utilization" score and compared across the three ethnic groups, the findings show significant differ-

Table 5.15
Comparison of Three Utilization Scales by Immigration Status

	Mean Rank		
Utilization Scales	Undocumented	Legalized	Test Statistic U
Resource $p < .05$, p. 89 (NS)	45.13	45.87	996.0
Comfort $p < .05^*$, p. 00	37.08	53.92	633.5*
Reluctance $P < .05^*$, p. 00	34.07	56.93	498.0*

Mann–Whitney U Test.
*Indicates a statistically significant difference.

ences by country of birth. The mean score for Haiti was significantly lower at 33.20 than El Salvador at 42.78 and Ireland at 60.52. A higher score indicates greater utilization (see Table 5.16).

In order to analyze further the meaning of the differences between the three countries on the "utilization" score, an analysis of variance (ANOVA) statistical test was used on undocumented Haitians, Irish, and Salvadorans only (see Table 5.17). There was a significant difference among the three undocumented groups on the combined utilization scale. Undocumented Haitians had the lowest score at 47.33 while Ireland had the highest at 86.33, meaning that Haitians with their highest level of need use the least services. When this same test was run on the three newly legalized immigrants, the Salvadorans used the least services with a mean score of 64.4, followed by the Haitians at 66.66 and the Irish with the highest mean score of 76.33, indicative of greater utilization.

Table 5.16
Kruskal–Wallis Comparison of Utilization Scale by Country of Birth

Scale	Mean Rank			Chi Square Statistic
	Haiti	Ireland	El Salvador	
Utilization	33.20	60.52	42.78	16.9032*

$p < 0.05$, *p. 00.

Table 5.17

Analysis of Variance of Utilization Scale among Undocumented Haitians, Irish, and Salvadorans

Undocumented Haitians N = 15		Undocumented Irish N = 15		Undocumented Salvadorans N = 15			
Mean	SD	Mean	SD	Mean	SD	Df	F Ratio
47.33	7.29	66.6	8.59	58.53	6.96	2	58.53*

p < .05, *p. 00.

When comparing undocumented Haitians with legalized Haitians, there was a 19-point difference in their mean scores (see Table 5.18). Undocumented Haitians had the lowest score, meaning less utilization. Likewise, the undocumented Irish had a lower mean score by ten points. The undocumented Salvadorans had a six-point difference between themselves and the legalized Salvadorans.

These results lend strong support to the second hypothesis; that is, that undocumented immigrant status is associated with less utilization of social services by the undocumented. On comparisons by country of birth, a pattern emerged in that the Irish immigrants had consistently higher scores on the utilization scales and the Haitians, despite their dire straits, had consistently low scores.

Several other individual utilization questions were asked of the undocumented immigrants in terms of their perception of eligibility, being asked for documentation as a prerequisite to services, use of health care services, and use of essential services such as the police and fire departments.

A comparison of responses by the undocumented and legalized groups in terms of their perceptions of their eligibility for services since IRCA is presented in Table 5.19. The results certainly indicate differences in their per-

Table 5.18

Analysis of Variance of Utilization Scale among Legalized Haitians, Irish, and Salvadorans

Legalized Haitians N = 15		Legalized Irish N = 15		Legalized Salvadorans N =15			
Mean	SD	Mean	SD	Mean	SD	Df	F Ratio
66.66	7.63	76.33	12.49	64.4	10.23	2	5.68*

p > .05, *p. 00.

ceptions about their eligibility, in that 44 percent of the undocumented believe themselves to be less eligible in comparison to 13 percent of the legalized. However, the majority of both groups indicate that they do not know their own eligibility.

When asked if, in the aftermath of IRCA, they seek more, the same amount, or fewer social services, the results pinpoint a significant difference in the responses of the undocumented compared with the legalized group. As shown in Table 5.20, the undocumented seek less services (31%) than the legalized group (11%). Undocumented immigrants that reported using more services was a meager 4.4 percent while the legalized indicated an increase at 22.2 percent. However, the most significant response from both the undocumented

Table 5.19
Responses of Undocumented and Legalized Immigrants on Eligibility since IRCA

Variable since IRCA	Undocumented N = 45		Legalized N = 45	
	Number	Percent	Number	Percent
don't know	19	42.2	20	44.4
more services	-	-	13	28.9
same amount	3	6.7	6	13.3
less services	20	44.4	6	13.3
other	3	6.7	-	-
Total	45	100.0	45	99.9 *

*Indicates a rounding error.

Table 5.20
Comparison of Responses on Seeking Services after the Passage of IRCA by Immigration Status

Since IRCA do you seek:	Undocumented		Legalized	
	Number	Percent	Number	Percent
more service?	2	4.4	10	22.2
the same amount?	8	17.8	9	20.0
less service?	14	31.1	5	11.1
don't know?	21	46.7	20	44.4
Total	45	100.0	44	97.7**

$\chi^2 = 10.67$*, p. 03, df = 4; **indicates a rounding error.

at 46 percent and the legalized at 44 percent was that they, once again, "did not know."

When asked, "If you seek less services, have you found other ways to meet your needs?" the results indicate that the undocumented are least successful in finding other ways to meet their needs (see Table 5.21). Of the undocumented, 15 percent responded "most of the time" as compared with the legalized group at 31.6 percent; 60 percent of the undocumented reported "some of the time" in comparison with the legalized at 39 percent.

When asked if they had been asked for documentation regarding their immigration status before receiving services, the results were roughly equal between the two groups. It is important to note that in Massachusetts at the time of the research there was an executive order barring state workers from inquiring about immigration status as a prerequisite to providing services. Given this fact, the "equal" results on the question of documentation was predicable. By the mid- and late 1990s, there had been an enormous negative shift in state attitudes toward the undocumented (see Table 5.22).

When comparisons were made in terms of responses to the question on use of public hospitals over the period of a year, the results indicate a significant difference in the responses of the undocumented in relation to the legalized group. The difference clearly points to less use of public hospitals by the undocumented (see Table 5.23). To the question, "Has concern about immigration status caused you to avoid getting help for yourself or your family over the past year?" 60.0 percent of the undocumented immigrants answered "yes," while 28.9 percent of the legalized responsed "yes."

Finally, when asked, "If you were a victim of a crime, would you report it?" 84 percent of the undocumented and 91 percent of the legalized answered in the affirmative. Again, when asked, "If you were aware of a fire or fire safety violations, would you report it?" 97 percent of the undocumented answered "yes," and 88 percent of the legalized answered in the affirmative as

Table 5.21

Comparison of Responses on Finding Other Ways to Meet Needs by Immigration Status

If you seek less services,have you found other ways to meet your needs?	Undocumented		Legalized	
	Number	Percent	Number	Percent
most of the time	5	15.2	12	31.6
some of the time	20	60.6	15	39.5
not at all	5	15.2	11	28.9
Total	30	91.0	38	100.0

Note: Number is less than 45/45 because the question was asked if they seek less services only.

$\chi^2 = 8.53^*$, p. 03, df = 3.

Table 5.22

Comparison of Responses on Being Asked for Documentation before Service by Immigration Status

	Undocumented		Legalized	
	Number	Percent	Number	Percent
yes	22	50.0	20	44.4
no	22	50.0	25	55.6
Total	44	100.0	45	100.0

$\chi^2 = 0.27$, p. 59, df = 1 (NS).

Table 5.23

Comparison of Responses on Use of Public Hospital over the Last Year

Has concern about immigration status caused you to avoid use of public hospitals over the last year?	Undocumented		Legalized	
	Number	Percent	Number	Percent
yes	27	60.0	13	28.9
no	18	40.0	32	71.1
Total	45	100.0	45	100.0

$\chi^2 = 8.82^*$, p. 00, df = 1.

well (see Tables 5.24 and 5.25). One suspects that these two last sets of responses may be indicative of the aching longing of both sets of immigrants to conform to the laws of their adopted homeland. Paradoxically, the qualitative findings on the undocumented will sketch quite a reverse picture: particularly among the Haitians and Salvadorans, a profile of fear of police and govern-

Table 5.24

Comparison of Responses on Reporting a Crime by Immigration Status

If you were a victim of a crime, would you report it?	Undocumented		Legalized	
	Number	Percent	Number	Percent
yes	38	84.4	41	91.1
no	7	15.6	4	8.9
Total	45	100.0	45	100.0

$\chi^2 = 0.93$, p. 33, df = 1 (NS).

Table 5.25
Comparison of Responses on Reporting a Serious Fire Violation by Immigration Status

If you were aware of a fire or serious fire safety violation, would you report it?	Undocumented		Legalized	
	Number	Percent	Number	Percent
yes	44	97.8	40	88.9
no	1	2.2	5	11.1
Total	45	100.0	45	100.0

$\chi^2 = 2.85$, p. 09, df = 1 (NS).

ment officials that mirrored the anguish occurring in their home countries at the time of the research.

FINDINGS ON RESPONSIVENESS OF THE SOCIAL SERVICE SYSTEM TO THE NEEDS OF THE UNDOCUMENTED

The third underlying assumption that guided the research stated that the impact of immigration status on the responsiveness of the social service system had been to detect the ability of the system to respond to the needs of the undocumented. The responsiveness scale that was developed to test this hypothesis asked the respondent to indicate to what extent a list of twenty-four specific services had been responsive to their needs. The categories of responses were "very helpful," "not helpful," and "have not sought services for this problem." The results on the responsiveness scale tend to disprove the third hypothesis: that the impact of undocumented status would be to reduce the responsiveness of the social services system. However, on other variables that measure responsiveness of the social service system, the results tend to confirm the third hypothesis. Findings indicate that there is not a statistically significant difference in the perception of the undocumented as compared with the legalized group on the responsiveness of the system to their needs.

When statistical tests (i.e., ANOVA) were run on the responsiveness scale by country of birth, the results indicated that there is a statistically significant difference in the responses by country of birth. Haiti had the highest mean score, with El Salvador next, and Ireland last, meaning that Haitians perceived the system to be more responsive by far than El Salvador or Ireland. At face, this appears to be an anomaly (see Table 5.26).

In order to analyze further the role that immigrant status was playing in relation to the three countries on the responsiveness scale, a statistical test was run on the undocumented Haitians, Irish, and Salvadorans (see Table 5.27) and the legalized Haitians, Irish, and Salvadorans (see Table 5.28). The

Table 5.26
Analysis of Variance Comparison of Responsiveness Scale by Country of Birth

	Haiti		Ireland		El Salvador			
	Mean	SD	Mean	SD	Mean	SD	Df	F Ratio
Responsiveness	21.56	10.42	8.70	8.57	15.76	9.77	2	13.461*

p < .05, *p. 00.
*Represents a statisticall significant difference.

results reveal that among the undocumented group, the undocumented Haitians have a far greater mean score than the Irish, and are four mean points higher than the Salvadorans. This higher mean score indicates that the Haitians and Salvadorans feel that the system is more responsive than the Irish undocumented (see Table 5.27).

Table 5.27
Analysis of Variance of Responsiveness Scale among Undocumented Haitians, Irish, and Salvadorans

	Undocumented Haitians N = 15		Undocumented Irish N = 15		Undocumented Salvadorans N = 15			
	Mean	SD	Mean	SD	Mean	SD	Df	F Ratio
Responsiveness	21.86	11.89	6.46	7.80	17.33	9.63	2	9.54*

p > .05, *p. 00 (Subset Haiti*, El Salvador*).

Table 5.28
Analysis of Variance of Responsiveness Scale among Legalized Haitians, Irish, and Salvadorans

Scale	Legalized Haitians N = 15		Legalized Irish N = 15		Legalized Salvadorans N = 15			
	Mean	SD	Mean	SD	Mean	SD	Df	F Ratio
Responsiveness	21.26	11.89	10.93	7.80	14.2	9.63	2	4.76*

p > .05, *p. 01 (Subset Haiti*).

In Table 5.28 we see once again that the legal Haitians also perceive the system to be more responsive. The mean scores for the undocumented and legal Haitians are nearly identical. Only among the Irish are the mean scores in the expected direction with the undocumented Irish with the lower score by about four points. Similar to the Haitians, the undocumented Salvadorans have a higher mean score than the legalized.

In sum, the test results do not confirm the third hypothesis by first of all indicating that there is not a significant difference between the undocumented and legalized groups on the responsiveness scale. Second, the tests by country of birth reveal the unanticipated finding that Haitians find the social service system more responsive than the other two ethnic groups. One possible explanation may lie in the high level of need in the Haitian group, which may impel them to seek more assistance from the system which in turn may help them to perceive it to be more responsive. In light of the Haitians' scores on reluctance factors in seeking services (their score was the lowest, meaning most reluctant), the findings on the responsiveness scale are confounding. However, the results of the qualitative data will provide some insight into this phenomenon.

Statistical tests were run on several individual variables that relate to the respondents' view of the impact of immigration status on the responsiveness of the system, experiences of having been turned away from services, and, if desperate, could they find services.

The results of a comparison of the response of the undocumented and legalized immigrants on the question of responsiveness of the system when asked, "Do you think because you are an immigrant the social service system has been less, more, or about the same as everyone else?" indicate that the undocumented find the system less responsive than the legalized group in a statistically significant way. This finding indicates that there are statistically significant differences in the responses of the undocumented as compared with the newly legalized group (see Table 5.29).

When the same variable is compared by country of birth (see Table 5.30), the results show that there is also a significant difference in the responses of the three countries. This time it is the Salvadorans that find the system less responsive. The results of a comparison of responses of undocumented and legal immigrants on the social service system after the passage of IRCA indicate that there is a significant difference in the responses of the undocumented group as compared with the legalized group. The undocumented perceive the system to be less responsive (see Table 5.31).

When undocumented immigrants were compared with legalized immigrants on the question of whether they or their family had been turned away from a public hospital, the answer from both groups was a resounding "no": 93 percent of the undocumented in this study had never been turned away from public hospitals. An impressive 95.6 percent of legalized immigrants also reported that they had never been turned away (see Table 5.32). In the light of

Table 5.29

Comparison of the Responsiveness of the System to Need by Immigration Status

Do you think because you are an immigrant the social service system has been more responsive, less responsive, or the same as everyone else?	Undocumented		Legalized	
	Number	Percent	Number	Percent
same as everyone	15	34.9	30	68.2
less responsive	28	65.1	14	31.8
Total	43	100.0	44	100.0

$\chi^2 = 12.41^*$, p. 00, df = 2.

Table 5.30

Comparison of the Responsiveness of the System to Need by Country of Birth

Do you think because you are an immigrant the social service system has been more responsive, less responsive, or the same as everyone else?	Haitians		Irish		Salvadorans	
	Number	Percent	Number	Percent	Number	Percent
same as everyone	15	53.6	22	73.3	8	27.6
less responsive	13	46.4	8	26.7	21	72.4
Total	28	100.0	30	100.0	29	100.0

$\chi^2 = 12.41^*$, p. 00, df = 2.

the 1996 immigration law restrictions, this finding is probably short lived. Last, the undocumented and newly legalized immigrants were asked the question, "If your life circumstances became totally desperate, could you find help in your local community?" The results indicate no statistical differences in the responses. Interestingly, the majority in both groups believe they could find services in a desperate situation: 70 percent of the undocumented and 82 percent of the legalized immigrants (see Table 5.33).

The results from the interview with the undocumented and newly legalized immigrants indicate that undocumented immigrants as a group have greater social and economic needs than their legalized counterparts. There were sig-

Table 5.31

Comparison of the Responsiveness of the System to Need since Passage of IRCA by Immigration Status

Since the passage of IRCA in 1986, do you believe that the social service system has been:

	Undocumented		Legalized	
	Number	Percent	Number	Percent
More responsive	9	20.5	16	35.6
About the same	19	43.2	26	57.8
Less responsive	16	36.4	3	6.7
Total	44	100.1**	45	100.1**

$\chi^2 = 11.93*$, p. 00, df = 2.

**Indicates a rounding error.

Table 5.32

Comparison of Experience of Being Turned Away from a Public Hospital by Immigtation Status

Have you or a member of your immediate family had the experience of being turned away from a public hospital when you sought services?	Undocumented		Legalized	
	Number	Percent	Number	Percent
Yes	3	6.8	1	2.2
No	41	93.2	43	95.6
Total	44	100.0	44	97.8*

$\chi^2 = 2.03$, p. 36, df = 2 (NS).

*Indicates a rounding error.

nificant differences across the three ethnic groups of immigrants; in particular, there was a consistent pattern of greater need among the Haitian immigrants. They showed the greatest disparity in relation to Irish immigrants. When viewing undocumented and legalized immigration status by the three different ethnic groups, the finding of greater need among the undocumented was confirmed most strongly among undocumented Haitians and Salvadorans. This would lead to the conclusion that other variables not measured in the research design may be playing a significant role, such as ethnicity, language, and level of education. Although no significant difference was observed on one of the scales measuring use of resources, the finding of significant differences on two other utilization scales leads to the conclusion that undocumented immigrants are

Table 5.33
Comparison of Responses on Finding Services if Situation is Desperate by Immigration Status

If your life circumstances became totally desperate, could you find help in your local community?	Undocumented		Legalized	
	Number	Percent	Number	Percent
Yes	31	70.5	37	82.2
No	13	29.5	8	17.8
Total	44	100.0	45	100.0

$\chi^2 = 1.70$, p. 19, df = 1 (NS).

less inclined to use social services than their legalized counterparts. These findings differ across the three ethnic groups, following a pattern where the Haitians are the least comfortable in using services as are the Salvadorans. The Irish appear to be the most likely to utilize services. This finding of less utilization among the undocumented was confirmed across each of the three ethnic groups as well, leading to the conclusion that undocumented immigrants use fewer services despite their increased need.

Although the finding on the responsiveness scale was not significant, there were differences between the undocumented and the legalized on other individual variables used to measure responsiveness. On the responsiveness scale, the answer chosen most often in the twenty-four-item scale was "have not sought help with these problems." One conclusion that can be drawn from this is that the responsiveness of the system has not yet been tested by immigrants as a group. The high score on the responsiveness scale (meaning greater responsiveness) that the Haitians attained and their low utilization score remains an anomaly, particularly in the light of their answers on the other variables measuring responsiveness.

The quantitative findings from this study reveal that the undocumented population has increased social and economic needs that are directly associated with their undocumented status. There were significant differences on three out of the four social need scales, meaning that the undocumented showed greater need in terms of depression, stress, health, and drug and alcohol use in comparison with the legalized group. On the three economic need scales, housing, financial well-being, and workplace abuse, the undocumented group again showed greater need than the legalized group on all three scales. When the social needs of undocumented persons were compared across the three countries of origin, undocumented persons from Haiti had the highest need score, followed by those from El Salvador. Likewise, on the economic need scales, Haitians and Salvadorans had the highest needs. The next section provides a more nuanced and texturized panorama of the world of the undocumented through the eyes of providers of services to them.

KEY INFORMANT INTERVIEWS OF PROVIDERS OF SERVICES TO THE UNDOCUMENTED

A second survey, a key informant interview with providers of services to the undocumented from a variety of disciplines, was utilized as a validity check on the undocumented and legalized immigrants' questionnaire and as a means of providing texture and context to the treacherous terrain and lives of the undocumented in the aftermath of IRCA.

Criteria used to select service providers were (1) expert knowledge of the undocumented population from at least one of the cultural groups under study, (2) a working understanding of IRCA and implications for undocumented immigrants and their families, (3) an in-depth perspective on the social and economic needs of immigrant groups, and (4) knowledge of the formal and informal service delivery system in the Boston area (i.e., public, private, formal, informal). From a list of agencies and programs that worked with the undocumented, a sample of fifteen key informants was drawn up based on their understanding of either the Haitian, Irish, or Salvadoran community and those willing to be interviewed on the sensitive and politically volatile issue of undocumented immigrants. The participants were assured that no person or agency would be identified in the study; only aggregate content analysis would be done. Participants came from two community health centers, an immigrant hotline service, several multiservice centers, a public health center, a mental health center, a legal firm serving immigrant groups, an advocacy group, and two church-related services. The intent was to maximize representativeness by choosing providers from across three different ethnic groups and from different "angles" of service provision—that is, social work, legal aid, health care, and psychological services. In sum, the key informant sample included:

- a public health social worker (for Haitians)
- a Haitian administrator
- a Hispanic administrator
- a mental health worker (for Haitians)
- a psychologist (for Haitians)
- a Salvadoran administrator
- a Salvadoran community organizer
- an immigration lawyer (all groups)
- an Irish administrator
- an immigration legal counsel agency (all groups)
- an Irish outreach worker
- an administrator of an immigration advocacy group (all groups)
- an administrator of a multiservice agency (Haitians)

- a hotline worker (Irish)
- an Irish social worker from a community health center (all groups)

The structured interview questionnaire consisted of twenty-six open-ended items. The first set of questions related to the question of differences in the needs of undocumented immigrants before the implementation of IRCA and after, in seven specific areas: health, housing, job conditions, income, employment, marital and family relations, drug and alcohol use, and psychological well-being. A second set of questions related to utilization of social services by undocumented immigrants in the aftermath of the implementation of IRCA, gaps in needed services, the undocumented immigrant's comfort or discomfort in seeking services, and the kinds of services available to the undocumented. A third set of questions probed for answers regarding the responsiveness of the social service system to the needs of the undocumented after full implementation of IRCA. Last, several questions asked if the undocumented are leaving the country as a result of the implementation of IRCA or other factors, whether employers understand the rights and obligations of the employer sanctions provision of IRCA, what might some of the implications be for the children of the undocumented into the future, what needs to be done to improve the situation of the undocumented, and what lessons can be gleaned from the 1986 immigration legislation.

Since each of the key informants had an investment as a service provider to the undocumented, there would certainly be a proimmigrant stance in the findings as well as the possibility of bias since each key informant knew the purpose of the study was to surface the human toll of the 1986 law on specific undocumented immigrants.

FINDINGS FROM THE KEY INFORMANTS INTERVIEWS

Two paradoxical views held by the undocumented population that kept coming up in the interviews form the dominant theme of this analysis: fear versus hope. On the one hand, there is a stark, day-to-day, "looking over their shoulders" type of fear that has been intensified by the passage of employer sanctions. Then, on the other hand, there is evidence of a tenacious stubborn hope that something will happen to allow the undocumented to regularize their immigration status. For many of them, their task is to do two things: first of all, to survive, and then to do nothing to jeopardize any potential they may have in the future to become legalized.

Categories that emerged from the data generated through the interviews were the general impact of IRCA on the undocumented, social and economic needs of the undocumented, utilization of services by the undocumented, responsiveness of the local social service system, and cross-cultural differences. The constant comparative method for qualitative data analysis was used to analyze the key informant responses (Glazer and Strauss 1967).

GENERAL IMPACT OF IRCA AND THE EXPERIENCE
OF BEING UNDOCUMENTED

Phrases that kept surfacing in the interviews when informants were describing the current situation of undocumented immigrants were: "no options," "fearful," "being on high alert," "backs against the wall," "lives on hold," and "pushed to the brink." Reflecting on the general impact of IRCA on the undocumented, one social worker stated the case this way:

> I think what IRCA did was it publicly frightened people. It brought out something people knew was there but it added the notion that the INS was everywhere.

The incident of an INS raid on Suffolk Downs race track that culminated in the arrest of many undocumented Central Americans was recounted by many of the key informants:

> Those people were sleeping in tack rooms and in stables with the horses.
> Outreach worker

What IRCA did, said another informant, was

> to make public what people knew privately in the underground . . . that the undocumented exist.
> Irish worker

Nearly every informant spoke of an intensification of needs among the undocumented reflective of the impact of IRCA, not so much by itself, but in combination with the economic downspin in the 1980s and early 1990s. Every service provider was extremely conscious that the "Massachusetts miracle" had fizzled, and in its wake there has been an atmospheric change in attitudes toward the undocumented. There was a keen awareness that in times of flatness in the economic marketplace, vulnerable populations such as the undocumented feel the effects first. One informant analyzed the situation of the undocumented this way:

> I'll tell you what is interesting about the undocumented population. I find in my experience that if there are cracks in the system, they fall into them faster than anyone else.
> Community health worker

Another worker put it this way:

> The difference for the undocumented at this point is the intensity of the problems because they don't have even the option to look for work.
> Mental health worker

In 1985 in Massachusetts, then, Governor Michael Dukakis issued Executive Order 257 which said that state workers and state agencies were not to ask for the legal status of any client as a prerequisite for state services. By 1991, then, Governor William Weld had eliminated the undocumented from eligibility for general relief. As to the fate of Executive Order 257, providers of services feared to invoke it lest it be repealed. One Haitian social worker said cryptically, "Executive Order 257 has been gutted." Nearly every provider mentioned that removing the undocumented from general relief had a broad chilling effect on the entire undocumented community.

A Salvadoran worker spoke of the Salvadoran community watching the 1992 United States presidential campaign on television:

> The stronger the Buchanan campaign got, the more we worried that they would not extend our TPS [temporary protected status] because of the anti-immigrant sentiment.

Nearly every informant spoke of what the experience of being an undocumented immigrant is like. As the interviewer, I was constantly aware of how close some of the key informants were to the experience of being undocumented. Some recounted their own experience as an undocumented immigrant. In one instance, the informant, who was a Salvadoran administrator, spoke about the legalization program and of the experience of a woman who arrived a matter of days after the 1982 cutoff point and, therefore, could not be legalized. As he spoke of her experience of being undocumented to "this very day," he added, "and that woman, she is my mother."

In attempting to describe the pervasiveness of the fear of the undocumented, a social worker from a community center described her experience with one client:

> I had her in therapy for two and a half years, and about six months ago, she told me she was registered under a false name. I never knew she was undocumented.
>
> Irish caseworker

Needs of the Undocumented

Housing

In general, the needs of the undocumented described in the interviews were very basic, survival types of needs such as the need for housing, food, health care, jobs, and money. However, across the three ethnic groups, there were considerable variations in the intensity of the need. The Haitians experience homelessness, while the Salvadorans in the main do not. The Irish report no housing problems nor any homelessness, while the Salvadorans and the Haitians report marked exploitation by landlords with no legal recourse.

A public health key informant described housing conditions among the Haitians as "horrible": overcrowding, abusive landlords, broken windows, broken heaters.

> There is definitely less concern about keeping the basic standards of health in terms of housing. Very often the landlords know their tenants are undocumented and they don't worry about fixing the toilets, the bathtub, about having the kitchen functional within the health regulations, especially for gas leaks and stuff like that.
>
> Salvadoran worker

Income

There was a general sense that many of the undocumented after the implementation of employer sanctions lost their jobs and were scrambling for work in the informal job market as home-health aides, nannies, or housekeepers, or they tried their hand at being self-employed as street vendors. If they found another job, it was for less pay and no benefits.

When they were working, many undocumented individuals and families shared living space and the rent with other families. When they lost their jobs, they ended up going from place to place within a friendship network that for many, over time, wore thin.

As one administrator described it,

> The general impression that I get is that those that were employed were able to bring in some income prior to IRCA. Those who have been let go by their employers are now dependent on friends and families for housing and for all of their other needs.
>
> Haitian administrator

Marital and Family Relations

Several informants spoke of the strain on marital relations where one partner is undocumented and the other is legal, particularly if the undocumented person is male and unemployed and is unable to contribute financially to the family. In general, when two persons are living together, a pattern of blame occurs when there is not enough income coming in from one party because he or she is undocumented. Others spoke of the extreme stress that the undocumented community suffers. For some, the emotional vacuum they experience in the United States comes about because their family has remained behind, for example, in El Salvador. One informant spoke of undocumented persons spending their whole month's paycheck on telephone calls to El Salvador. Relating to the general stress of the undocumented, a Hispanic administrator said, "It's really very, very hard for anybody to keep any level of sanity when they have no options and when they feel trapped."

A Haitian public health worker spoke of the emotional strain for Haitians who have left family behind in Haiti with the intent of supporting them financially:

> It is very difficult for the people who have the responsibility and the desire to send money back to kin in Haiti knowing they won't get what they need unless they do this and not being able to get work because of the difficulty of IRCA.

Health-Related Concerns

In general, the informants spoke of the psychic numbness and emotional deadness that takes over in some of the undocumented. Informants from all three ethnic groups spoke of the use of alcohol as a coping device among the undocumented. An Irish outreach worker spoke of his experience regarding undocumented Irish's use of alcohol:

> A lot of time when we have special events coming off I would spend the morning going around to all the Irish pubs with the posters. In the winter time I always noticed that they're packed in the mornings with Irish people who I'd recognize who are undocumented and out of work. There have to be problems there.

A mental health worker spoke of the problem of loss of income and no coverage for medications among the undocumented:

> The problem that we have seen is that you have the medical needs of the undocumented escalate because they don't purchase medication. People who have high blood pressure, or who are psychotic who have medication to stabilize them, or if they have diabetes.

A Haitian public health worker spoke of the futility of not providing health services to the undocumented:

> We have a lot of people living in crowded conditions where tuberculosis is the most serious problem, and it's interesting in terms of being mean spirited towards the undocumented population. It's ironic, actually you're putting everyone at risk.

One public health worker gave an example of a poignant, "unreasonable" hope among her clients. Some of her clients had tested positive for AIDS. They were in extreme medical need and therefore were able to qualify for Medicaid. The clients did not want to go on Medicaid but wanted to hold onto the hope of regularizing their immigration status and therefore did not want to become public charges. This existed in the face of almost certain death.

Workplace Abuse

In relating to the impact of employer sanctions, informants told stories of the undocumented being fired, even the ones who had been "grandfathered" under IRCA, having wages withheld, and being asked for green cards instead of the I-9 required documents; but they also spoke of undocumented persons working in legitimate industries and paying taxes because they had "passed" as legalized. A Haitian worker spoke of an employer of a cleaning firm demanding documents from undocumented workers while at the same time she herself was in the business of selling false documentation.

In describing the impact of employer sanctions, many informants linked its effect to the overall economy:

> The economy has affected people who are legal, it has doubly affected people who are undocumented. Once you have a downturn in the economy you are left with the service industry . . . maybe.
>
> Immigration lawyer

A Hispanic social worker described the downward spiral that occurs for many of the undocumented:

> We have many people who altogether [sic] rent an apartment, you know a group of Salvadorans or Guatemalans, they would rent an apartment and they fix it and they all pay the rent together. They work and they clean and they're really productive members of society if you want to look at it that way. Now they get kicked out of their jobs because of employer sanctions and they are unable to pay the rent, so they are out there going from friend to friend until they reach the streets and the shelter.
>
> Hispanic agency

Utilization of Services

In some ways, the part of the interview that focused on utilization of services by the undocumented was cut short by one oft-repeated, rapid-fire question: "What services?"

Aside from WIC, Healthy Start, and AFDC, if the children have been born in the United States, there were no public services for the undocumented.

Increasingly even the WIC program for pregnant women is becoming more difficult for undocumented women to access. The program requires women to provide documentation on her income and the father of the child. Often the father does not want to provide income certification or cannot, and this places the undocumented woman and her child at risk. Beyond this, there is the generalized confusion that exists in the community around the possibility of being seen as someone "likely to become a public charge." The guiding rule for the undocumented is to do nothing that will jeopardize their chances for regularizing their immigrant status. In the interest of this, the undocumented err on the side of caution and forego using services. Even providers of services are cautious.

> We are happy when we see people not having to use services because it means that the possibility of becoming a public charge is reduced.
>
> Irish social worker

Several informants spoke of the confusion about "cash benefit" programs. Because the undocumented are so focused on not being seen as a public charge, they are under the impression that public welfare includes AFDC, Healthy Start, and WIC, which in reality it does not.

The undocumented will utilize the free health care pool at city hospitals as well as legal services if they are provided by a "trustworthy" group such as a church (e.g., their local parish), neighborhood organizations, or other groups that they feel they can trust.

On the other hand, certain kinds of services will not be used by the undocumented. As one legal service agency administrator noted,

> If it is bureaucratic, government-related, unfamiliar to them in terms of structures or systems, culturally unfamiliar, or not linguistically accessible, there is great resistance to utilize.

Relating to the same point, a Haitian administrator stated,

> Oh, they would stay away from any type of anything that they see as the law, the police or the government. They're very scared.

Before IRCA, among Haitians, adult education was a service that the undocumented were attracted to and utilized. As one Haitian agency administrator indicated:

> We used to love enrolling as many undocumented people as possible, seeing this as a wonderful service to help them get ready for the time when they would straighten out their situation and quickly become productive persons.

After IRCA, because of the federal trickle of funding into the Adult Literacy Contract, the undocumented could not apply. Several providers spoke of service contracts and the new stress on accountability, on performance outcomes, and on the demand for personal information that was somewhat intrusive. All these have conspired to effectively filter out the undocumented clients from the service circuit. As one administrator observed:

> The federal government certainly doesn't want the tax dollars to serve the undocumented. We had to throw up our hands and say, these are the

programs that are going to be funded, and there's very little that we can do now for the undocumented.

Services that the undocumented prefer are generally in a collective or group mode of bringing information or services to them. Food pantries and other such programs provide a needed service and allow the undocumented to remain anonymous. One community health care worker spoke of undocumented Irish immigrants coming in for health care services with false names and social security numbers, and when they were asked to fill out agency information forms, they would excuse themselves to the bathroom and then would flee out the back door. Fear of exposure of their undocumented status affects the ability of the undocumented to use services such as day care as well.

> We used to have many undocumented families in the day care. But now the information that they want, the social security numbers to check income levels, this is too much information for the undocumented to give to get service.
>
> Haitian administrator

Several informants spoke of the undocumented's unwillingness to use AFDC for their children born in the United States, lest for some reason the connection between themselves and the children would work against them in terms of trying to alter their immigration status.

Responsiveness of the System to the Needs

One of the most refreshing aspects of the key informant interviews was hearing first-hand about the responsiveness and inventiveness of community-based providers of services to the undocumented within the ethnic communities that they serve. One Salvadoran administrator spoke of the efforts of his agency to address the current needs of the undocumented in ways that require no public or agency money to initiate:

> Our agency formed a food coop about a year ago and the idea back then was that many people were cut off from food stamps, were unemployed because of not being documented. So what we found is if we could pool resources from the community, we could begin buying food, the food that we need, you know, beans, rice, basic food staples, buy lots and resell them to ourselves at a very low price.

He went on to describe the way it works and to state that "these are community-based, community-initiated ways to deal with the problem of lack of resources. We have not done anything from a financial point of view. Only that of encouraging one of our workers to actively support the project." Next, they are beginning a project on a cleaning workers cooperative. This project stemmed from the fact that many of the undocumented were getting "ripped off" by employers who hired them by contract, but after they had completed their work, they were not paid. The agency decided to buy cleaning equipment themselves and look for contracts with organizations to do office cleaning and residential cleaning. The administrator was convinced that this model of help for the undocumented is the most workable and helpful, given the many constraints surrounding government resources.

Speaking to the issue of responsiveness to the needs of the undocumented, one administrator spoke of the ability of the nonprofit private sector being in the best position to serve the needs of the undocumented in the present economic climate:

> If private agencies are not receiving government funds and if they are able to structure their own programs, then those agencies can be responsive. I should say remain the most responsive. They've traditionally been the agencies serving the poorest of the poor, and they can remain true to that mission.

Within the public sector, agencies given kudos by the key informants for their responsiveness to the undocumented included Cambridge Hospital and Boston City Hospital:

> Most of the Haitians tend to use Boston City Hospital, they have been good to the undocumented because usually they do not ask them questions about their immigration status.
>
> Haitian administrator

Other public sector providers, said one social worker, noted for their efforts on behalf of immigrants and the undocumented were the City of Boston, the City of Somerville, and the City of Cambridge, for providing, or *trying* to provide,

> services to linguistic minorities, to refugees, and immigrants in a broad sweep including everybody, whether or not they're documented.
>
> Immigration legal services

Commenting that the good will is there on the part of providers to help the undocumented, but that the funding stream is nonexistent, one Hispanic administrator pointed out,

> At the meetings you go to everything is like forget the undocumented, we're trying to save the skills training, we're trying to save day care, and everything is tied, not everything, but many programs are tied to welfare so that those people who are out of the welfare system, they're out of the loop.
>
> Hispanic agency

One worker mused on the value of the WIC and Healthy Start programs:

> I must say that the two programs that are most favorable and that we use
> mostly are Healthy Start and WIC and we don't want the Republicans to
> know about it.

Cross-Cultural Differences

While the intensification of need among undocumented immigrants as a result of the passage of IRCA was consistent across the three ethnic groups in the
interviews so also the differences between the three groups were apparent.

Much of the data from the interviews suggest that having "no options" or
"feeling trapped" is a gnawing problem among the undocumented. For the Irish,
clearly the exception, the data suggests that they have more options than their
Haitian and Salvadoran counterparts. As one Irish social worker put it,

> I think they (the Irish) always know that they can always get a plane
> home and have a place to stay with their family and be able to draw on
> the dole until they find a job or something like that.

The circumstances for undocumented Haitians are in stark contrast given
the worsening economic, social, and political conditions in Haiti. One Haitian social worker stated,

> They're certainly not going back to Haiti at this point, so I'd say that
> most people are trying to make the best of it here. In Haiti, there is tre-
> mendous uncertainty, anxiety, very few people are working at this point,
> the schools are shut down.

For undocumented Salvadorans, a fragile peace remains in effect in their
homeland. Thus far, most Salvadorans are remaining in the United States.
One informant spoke of the "quantum leap" change for the undocumented in
coming to the United States from rural El Salvador:

> Hot water was simply out of the question before coming here. Even the
> lousy apartments have most often hot water running through the pipes.
> So the change, it is a quantum leap—I mean in their standard of life. In
> their home country they were making $20 a month, they couldn't give edu-
> cation to their children, or even clothes. Here they may well be oppressed in
> the standards measured here but from their point of view they are not. They
> want to stay here and that is understandable from a human point of view.
>
> Salvadoran administrator

Closer to home in Massachusetts, one Irish social worker spoke of differences
in job opportunities among the undocumented based on racial differences:

In Boston, for some people an Irish person is an acceptable person for everybody. Probably an Irish undocumented immigrant will get a job over a Haitian. And that's one of our concerns, for as much as we delight to see our people get jobs, we don't want people to get jobs at the expense of a Haitian, and the big danger is that in an economy like this, immigrants are pitted against one another. We have an informal job bank and probably will get a call because they want nice, white, Irish people to help.

Irish agency

Several Irish informants noted that in areas such as getting drivers' licenses from the Department of Motor Vehicles, "passing" into legitimate industry as legal employees, or trying to deal with the INS, access to help is facilitated when the service employee can identify with the ethnicity of the applicant. This of course can work in reverse when there is no similarity in ethnic identity.

Summary of Findings from Key Informant Interviews

- The impact of employer sanctions on the undocumented population has been to intensify the needs of this segment of the immigrant population.
- The implementation of employer sanctions in conjunction with the downspin in the economy in the 1980s and early 1990s has together worsened the circumstances of the undocumented.
- The larger community had been alerted to the invisible presence of the undocumented in part through the implementation of employer sanctions which required producing documentation for I-9 forms for all new employees.
- Job insecurity, loss of jobs, and workplace abuse had worsened among the undocumented in the wake of employer sanctions.
- Services to the undocumented had been greatly restricted as a result of the passage of IRCA, through restrictions on use of social services funded through federal monies and cuts in services at the state level.
- Fear of discovery of their legal status and the desire to avoid being seen as "in danger of becoming a public charge" dominates the day-to-day decisions of the undocumented.
- The undocumented had become increasingly cautious about using services that might jeopardize their ability to attain legal status.
- In the public sector, undocumented immigrants had used WIC, Healthy Start, AFDC (if their children have been born in the United States), and free health care pools at hospitals.
- In general, there is a fear and distrust of government services and contact with police.
- The undocumented population appears to be acutely vulnerable to economic and political shifts.
- The immigrant-serving community has been inventive in attempting to serve the undocumented, but have been curtailed in general by lack of agency funds.

• Several respondents indicated that undocumented Haitians are not returning to Haiti, nor are the Salvadorans returning to El Salvador. The Irish appear to have more options in terms of returning to Ireland.

• Some informants spoke of racial and ethnic differences in the Boston area and how they intensify the negative impact of IRCA on minority groups.

The findings from the interviews with the key informants provides insight into the many variables that affect the ability of the social service system to respond to the needs of the undocumented. This data underscores the fact that undocumented immigration is a "hairline trigger" issue easily set off by reversals in the economy, a rise in crime rates, or shifts in the political matrix. The general sense that one gets from the key informant interviews on the undocumented is that they are "on hold," "trapped," "without options," and on "high alert." In terms of service needs, the undocumented fall through the cracks in the system first and are wholly absorbed in basic survival needs. In housing, jobs, and other matters, exploitation without legal recourse is a daily fact of life for them. When employed, it is in the secondary or the informal market for less pay and no benefits except if they have "passed" as legal workers. The undocumented are dependent on the kindness of family and friends until this avenue runs dry. Shelters, and then the descent into the streets, become the final resource for many. Their poignant hope, despite all evidence that they will be able to regularize their immigration status, prevents them from seeking needed services and medications for fear of appearing to be "likely to become a public charge."

Acute pressures on the undocumented include the expectation of financial help by family members in their home countries, the "psychic numbness" and "emotional deadness" that many experience, and the tensions in households where one spouse is legalized and the other undocumented. The key informant responses verify that the undocumented have been filtered out of the social service system and also shows the inventiveness of some immigrant service communities in pooling their resources in a self-help model for the purpose of food and jobs. Finally, the differential impact of IRCA on the Irish as different from that of the Haitian and Salvadorans was amply identified. When viewed in light of their ineligibility for federally funded social services, the cuts that had reduced state social service funding, and their fear of "becoming a public charge" or being discovered and deported, the undocumenteds' view of the system as unresponsive would not be all that surprising.

The findings from both the interviews with the undocumented and the legalized immigrants and the key informant questionnaire reveal that some groups of undocumented immigrants are more vulnerable than other undocumented immigrants in terms of their social and economic needs. Undocumented Haitians are a case in point. Their high scores in terms of their social and economic needs are indicative of greater need. The low scores of undocumented Irish on the same scales suggest that undocumented Haitians may be carrying other burdens beyond being undocumented, such as race and language differences. Not surprising, the scores of undocumented Salvadorans on the social and economic need scales were considerably higher than that of the undocumented Irish. The Salvadorans also carry the burden of race and language difference.

The results in this research document the differential impact of IRCA on the nonwhite participants. These results are consistent with the history of immigration policy in the United States, where beneath a general pattern of ambivalence toward new immigrants lies a more specific, deeply ingrained pattern of racism and discrimination toward nonwhite immigrants. Undocumented immigrants experience the impact of IRCA "on top of" their own migration experience: the isolation and marginalization resulting from their undocumented status, language, culture, and differences in social organization. If they are racially or ethnically different from the dominant group, they experience first-hand America's own brand of pervasive racism. In light of this it is not surprising that Haitian and Salvadoran undocumented immigrants felt the effects of IRCA more acutely than their white counterparts.

Romano Mazzoli, cosponsor of IRCA, spoke of the legalization program as a "generous, encompassing, and compassionate bill," and Alan Simpson, the other sponsor, spoke of the legalization program as a means of removing "a fearful, easily exploitable subclass from our society" (in Meissner and Papademetriou 1988, p. 3). The results documented in this research demonstrate that the legalization program has certainly failed to be "generous," "encompassing," and "compassionate" in terms of the large number of undocumented immigrants "left behind" in the legalization process. When the employer sanctions provision was then imposed on this subclass of undocumented immigrants, their plight became all the more desperate and furtive.

Throughout the legislative history of IRCA, warnings were sounded about the implications for the broader community of permitting "the build-up of an underclass society living outside the protection of the law" (Fuchs, in Glazer 1985, p. 21). Among the concerns was the obvious abridgement of due process for the undocumented, the fact that immigration laws should not become themselves a means of engendering lawlessness, and the belief that a democracy cannot long flourish with a large population of rightless, powerless individuals living within its borders. This research documents their continued presence within the United States and the negative impact of IRCA on their social and economic needs, as well as their reluctance to use social services, and it provides insight into the inability of the local service system to respond to their needs. The magnification of their negative circumstances in the aftermath of the 1996 legislation can only be described as staggering. Anthony Lewis of the *New York Times* described the new law as one of "exquisite cruelty" (1997, p. A35).

When viewed in the light of America's historic treatment of new immigrant groups, the overall findings are not surprising but speak instead of an opportunity lost to redeem some of America's past xenophobic treatment of new immigrant groups which has been amply described in Chapter 2. The specific differential impact of IRCA on racial and ethnic undocumented immigrants verified in this study is all the more disquieting in view of the nation's attempts since the mid-1960s to rid domestic and immigration policy of racism and discrimination. This research suggests that the IRCA legislation has become a contemporary means of discrimination. The research provides evidence about the significance of immigration status in identifying needs and utilization of services among immigrant populations. On all but one measure of social and economic need, the undocumented scored higher than the legalized group. These findings are all the more impressive when compared across the three ethnic groups, since measures of ethnic and racial differences consistently placed Haitians in the greatest need and Irish immigrants consistently with least needs by comparison. Even then the needs of undocumented Irish immigrants were found to be significantly greater than legalized Irish immigrants. The same conclusion can be drawn from the measures of utilization of social services among undocumented immigrants, which were significantly lower than their legalized counterparts. Evidently even the presence of a larger population of legal Haitian, Irish, and Salvadoran communities in the Boston area with their varying levels of social support for the undocumented among them, was not sufficient to save them from the furtive exercise in survival that their lives had become.

While the debate on the existence of a large undocumented population within the United States remains a complex, volatile, and even incendiary political issue, "how we treat these human beings once they are in our midst" remains a test of the national character (Mahoney 1994, p. 587). Long ago, in a protracted ignoble episode when we had become economically dependent on the slave trade, the pattern of rationalization that took place was that slaves were, after all, only three-fifths of a person. When the United States denies basic human and civil rights to the undocumented today, are we not in grave danger of denying them their humanity, and in the process are we not degrading our own by creating in our own time what Williamson refers to as a "servile caste of serfs" (1996, p. 181).

NOTES

1. The Mann–Whitney U test is a counterpart of the t-test used to test differences between two independent samples. The Mann–Whitney U test is used on ordinal level, nonparametric data when the assumptions of the t-test cannot be met—namely, that the sample populations are normal or bell shaped in form and have equal variance. The U test ranks all the cases in order of increasing size and computes the test statistic U, the number of times a score from the first group precedes a score from the

second group. If the U test score is statistically significant, the "bulk" of scores in one population is higher than the bulk of scores in the other population (Borg and Gall 1989, pp. 356, 357, 564, 565).

2. A one-way analysis of variance was performed as a means of measuring whether the ethnic groups differed significantly among themselves on the five variables being studied. If the test yields a significant F ratio (the ratio of between-group variance to within-group variance), then it can be said that the groups differ significantly among themselves on the variable being studied (Borg and Gall 1989, pp. 355, 356).

Chapter 6

The Human Toll:
Scars on the
American Conscience

If a free society cannot help the many who are poor, it cannot save the few who are rich.

John F. Kennedy

Threading back through the theme of ambivalence that runs through this book, we see a historic, xenophobic treatment of new immigrants laced together with an insatiable appetite for cheap labor. Over and again business interests triumphed over labor's concern that new immigrants displaced U.S. workers and have kept working conditions and wages depressed. We have seen government colluding with agribusiness in supplying a silent, docile labor force to increase profits. Over time this practice created unique avenues for future undocumented migration into the United States. Even as legal immigration was being curtailed due to nativistic fears for the ethnic and racial mix in America, government-sponsored *bracero* and H-2 programs continued to subsidize agribusiness, particularly in the southwest and California.

When fault lines began to appear in the logic of the "need" to import foreign labor, for example in times of high unemployment, these programs were terminated, but foreign laborers would continue to risk clandestine entry into the United States in search of jobs and new lives.

Undocumented immigrants in the United States have been at one and the same time invisible and ubiquitous. They are ubiquitous in the sense that they can be found as textile and garment workers, as farm workers, fruit pickers, or stable hands, or lumber workers, construction workers, nannies, dish washers, hotel workers, hospital orderlies, housemaids, or in a variety of other secondary market jobs. Americans are quite ambivalent about our undocumented population. As consumers we benefit from their presence, but as citizens we insist that they have no right to be here and that further, it is they who are robbing us of tax-based benefits.

Concern for the human rights of the undocumented immigrants was raised for the first time in congressional debate on IRCA and formed part of the rationale for a generous, compassionate, and encompassing legalization program. Once undocumented immigrants were by and large legalized, employer sanctions would prevent future undocumented immigration by turning off the job magnet. The legislative history of IRCA showed how these two strategies, meant to work in concert, were ultimately cast in opposition to one another through carefully crafted compromises that ensured passage of IRCA but at the expense of coherence.

The objective of this book was to bring to light the fact that much of the undocumented population did not benefit from the 1986 legalization program. Cumulatively the research on the impact of the legalization and employer sanctions provisions documents the intensification of need that illegal immigrants experience, their resistance to use public services, and indeed, the lack of services that exist for them. In this sense, the research verified the fact that the undocumented are in a more dispossessed and desperate state than prior to the implementation of IRCA.

The overarching policy issue, therefore, is the continued presence of the undocumented in the underbelly of American society. This situation gives rise to two fundamental questions about IRCA: Without a generous legalization program and with the imposition of employer sanctions, was it the intent of Congress to create a policy of "starving out" the undocumented who were ineligible for legalization? Was serious thought given to the possibility that the undocumented, despite haunting, almost insurmountable difficulties, would still choose not to self-deport back to their home countries for a variety of reasons? Inexplicably, the findings in this study are consistent with America's historic xenophobic treatment of new immigrant groups but are at odds with the original intent of the Select Commission and at least Congress's expressed intent regarding this legislation.

A major premise here is that the compromises and ambiguities necessary to pass the central provisions of IRCA into law resulted in a lack of clarity regarding congressional intent which plagued the legalization provision during implementation and thus resulted in serious goal attenuation. In his book, *The Implementation Perspective: A Guide for Managing Social Service Delivery Programs*, Walter Williams alludes to this "lack of clarity and direction" from Congress. He notes that "this lack of specificity and consistency also comes about because programmatic detail is not an important commodity in Congress. Members often have little direct knowledge of how programs operate, scant time to acquire such knowledge, and no incentive for getting concerned with specifics" (1980, pp. 49, 50).

Williams also cites Greider's depiction that this ambiguity by Congress is purposeful and politically advantageous since Congress can claim credit for addressing social problems, but "they insulate themselves from direct responsibility for the hard decisions. . . . This allows them to second-guess the tough choices which they could not resolve among themselves" (1980, p. 50).

LeMay, in his book, *Analysis of a Public Policy: The Reform of Contemporary American Immigration Law*, looked at the many compromises made during the legislative phase of IRCA that, while necessary to passage, spelled trouble for the implementation phase. He notes that value dilemmas and conflicts remained unresolved in favor of compromise toward passage of the IRCA legislative package. These "conflicting values or goals" reemerged during the implementation phase when specific groups were charged with developing rules and regulations to accomplish the goal of the legislation (1994, p. 157).

Robert Mayer, in his book, *Policy and Program Planning: A Developmental Perspective*, points out that in implementation matters "when a given policy is complex or large in scale or when its planning and implementation are carried out by different bodies, elaboration is essential." While clarity in rules and regulations is important, Mayer also points out that, on the other hand, it is impossible and undesirable to have implementation procedures for large-scale policy actions that are so detailed and inflexible that adjustments for local conditions cannot take place. While a certain amount of local discretion bodes well for implementation, it can also be its "achilles heel" if responsibilities for implementation are delegated to different organizations or multiple levels of a large bureaucracy. What can occur is "considerable distortion in the intent of any plan" (1985, pp. 182, 183).

When applied to IRCA's legalization program, LeMay's and Mayer's insights strongly suggest fatal flaws in the implementation process. Although the legalization program was one law with one set of regulations, there was a great deal of decentralization to 107 local offices with varying levels of discretion in interpreting regulations in a flexible and generous manner or in an inflexible and rigid manner. North and Portes, in assessing the legalization program, referred to IRCA as a "long complicated bill . . . operating simultaneously within at least three groups of cultures: that of an American Bureaucracy, those of the immigrant-service agencies, and those of a variety of different foreign-born populations" (1988, p. 1).

Lessons learned from the implementation of IRCA's legalization program have to do with the large administrative and interpretive role given to the INS and its many local offices, with little time for reorienting themselves away from their primary enforcement function in immigration matters. The INS was attempting to implement the legalization provision with mixed messages around the question of just how generous Congress intended the legalization program to be or not be in granting amnesty to undocumented immigrants. Added to this, they were dealing with an unprecedented conservative cutoff date of nearly five years, excessive documentation requirements, the family unity dilemma, the lack of a broad-based educative process that actually "reached" the undocumented, and cost-prohibitive application fees and related costs.

The disparity that exists between policy formulation and policy outcomes within the legislative process usually ushers in yet another policy enactment with its own unintended or intended consequences. In the case of IRCA, the far more onerous and mean-spirited 1996 immigration law stands as stark proof of this eventuality.

THE DETERIORATING ENVIRONMENT
FOR THE UNDOCUMENTED

It has been more than fifteen years since the enactment of IRCA in 1986. Since undocumented immigrants are necessarily nameless and faceless, it is close to impossible to determine what the specific long-term effects of IRCA have been on them. The research in Chapter 5 furnishes a vivid picture of the short-term effects of IRCA on the undocumented. At this point, it is possible to gauge some attitudinal shifts in society at large through two windows: (1) new legislation directed toward the undocumented, and (2) media coverage on the more current situation of the undocumented.

In November 1994 Californian voters awoke to news that they had passed Proposition 187 by a 60-percent margin, a bill that required educators and medical professionals to deny public services to those suspected of being undocumented immigrants and to report them to the police. Although ultimately declared unconstitutional by the Supreme Court, Californians' approval of this mean-spirited bill sent a message to the rest of the country and to Washington in particular. In 1996, Congress picked up the "message" and passed the Illegal Immigration Reform and Responsibility Act of 1996. The earlier drafts of this legislation called for major reductions in the numbers of new legal immigrants, only to be whittled away by stakeholders such as immigrant advocacy groups and corporations, meaning that in effect there was no reduction in legal immigration. What remained in the bill were "stepped up," punitive measures toward the undocumented such as "removal of most of their rights of judicial appeal, a major increase in Border Patrol staffing and funding for a massive fence along parts of the Mexican Border and other high-tech means of interdiction." An antiterrorism act was also passed, which provided for immediate deportation of undocumented immigrants "without right of appeal." This bill was passed to coincide with the first anniversary of the Oklahoma City bombing even though no foreign-born person, legal or undocumented, had any connections to the actual perpetrator, Timothy McVeigh, our own homegrown terrorist. The 1996 immigration law is a curious piece of legislation in that it did not seek to prevent undocumented immigration by strengthening the central tool used in the 1986 immigration law (IRCA)—namely, the employer sanctions provision against employers who hire the undocumented ((Jonas and Thomas 1999, pp. vii, viii). Jonas, Thomas, and Isbister in the introduction to the book, *Immigration: A Civil Rights Issue for the Americas*, summarized the 1996 immigration law as not so much focused on reducing legal or undocumented immigration but rather riveted on "reducing and even in some cases eliminating their rights." They spell out their thesis in unequivocal terms:

The Congress seems to be pro-immigration but anti-immigrant. Taken together, what the most recent Acts indicate is that the representatives of the American people want a low-paid, compliant and easily exploitable immigrant labor force, with no basic democratic rights. (1999, p. viii)

Another deeply troubling issue raised by the current national and congressional debate on undocumented immigrants is the question of whether the Fourteenth Amendment of the Constitution should be repealed so that children of the undocumented born in the United States could be denied citizenship. A second, ancillary question that had arisen in public debate was whether the children of the undocumented should be barred from the public school system, thus overturning the 1982 Supreme Court ruling, *Doe v. Plyer*, on the issue. In the case of *Doe v. Plyer*, the court maintained that Texas, in bringing this suit, "was suffering the local effects of a national problem" (Hull 1983, p. 229). In its ruling, the court acknowledged that

When national immigration laws are not or cannot be enforced, it is the States, most particularly the Border States, that bear the heaviest burden. Nevertheless, the Court cannot suspend the operation of the Constitution to aid a State to solve its political or social problems. (Hull 1983, p. 229)

Other troubling questions directed specifically at legal immigrants include the question of whether the long-standing, hard-won principle of family reunification should be jettisoned from immigration policy. A second question revolved around rescinding AFDC, Medicare, and housing assistance for legal immigrants. Undocumented immigrants are already denied these benefits. The 1996 Welfare Reform Act has already denied elderly and disabled legal immigrants Supplementary Security Insurance (SSI) and food stamps. President Clinton tried to cushion part of this devastating act by ensuring that "the SSI Provision did not apply to immigrants whose status was affirmed before August 22, 1996," but the cutoff of food stamps was left unchanged (Jonas and Thomas 1999, p. viii).

It may be that the strain of absorbing new legal immigrants as well as the undocumented has heightened indignation leveled at illegal immigrants. Their "political powerlessness and clandestine existence," according to Hull, "render them natural scapegoats" (1983, p. 226). The larger issue may well be the transformative effect that immigration is having on "the social structure of the U.S."—namely, the gradual change "from a white country with several minority groups into a genuinely multicultural country in which no ethnic group will prevail" (Isbister 1999, p. 85).

The next section focuses on several national newspaper articles published in the late 1990s and at the turn of the century that deal with the impact of undocumented immigration along the border states but from the vantage point of the price tag that the undocumented pay.

In an August 24, 1997, *New York Times* article from El Paso, entitled "Silent Deaths Climbing Steadily as Migrants Cross Mexican Borders," the author, Sam H. Verhovek, reported that over the prior four years, "1,185 people had drowned, died of exposure or dehydration or been hit by automobiles while . . . trying to cross the border away from designated checkpoints" (p. 1). In the same article, Nestor Rodriguez from the Center for Immigration Research at Houston University, describes this phenomenon: "It's the equivalent of a large plane load of people crashing every year. But they do not all die at once, so these are like invisible, silent deaths" (p. 1). The article goes on to describe "a group of Mexican citizens trying to enter the country through an underground drainage pipe" (pp. 1, 18). When a fast-moving rainstorm filled the pipe with water, five men and one woman died.

The number of deaths along the two-thousand-mile Mexican–American border "has risen so greatly" that the INS has begun a campaign of "Stay Out, Stay Alive" for TV and newspaper ads in Mexico and other countries (Verhovek 1997, p. 18). What this campaign fails to take into account is the push factor: the abject poverty that the undocumented are trying to escape. Until this root cause of migration is addressed, undocumented immigrants will continue to risk their lives for the sake of life itself.

"The much-publicized crackdown by the Border Patrol [along the Mexican–American Border has had the effect of] prompting many immigrants to take increasingly circuitous and dangerous routes in their bid to make it to the United States" (Verhovek 1997, p. 18). Smugglers who lead the undocumented across the border, once paid, quickly abandon them to the miles and miles of desert, scrubland, or the treachery of the mountains.

A second *New York Times* article entitled "Boom Turns Border to Speed Bump," noted that since 1998, a small desert town in Agua Prieta, Mexico, has become the busiest border crossing along the two-thousand-mile spread between Mexico and the United States. In one night alone, 1,410 undocumented immigrants were rounded up before they could make their way across the border to Douglas, Arizona. In one month, 14,664 undocumented migrants were detained as compared with half that number the prior year. Border patrol agents have been refortified from four thousand in the mid-1990s to its current nine thousand. "Demographers say the crackdown has not slowed

the river of humanity crossing the southwest border but has re-channeled it."
This rechanneling has, however, made it "more dangerous. . . . Migrants now
die in greater numbers of thirst, hunger, sunstroke or cold. Others drown in
irrigation canals" (Dillon 2000, p. A4). Mexican government statistics indicate that 717 undocumented immigrants died in this area since 1995. It is
ironic that at a time when the United States is spending a record amount of
money to keep undocumented workers out, never has the booming economy
needed them more. Immigration scholar Wayne Cornelius notes that

Mexican immigrants are filling niches that employers can't even try to fill with American workers. So even though migrants must expose themselves to life-threatening
hazards, they'll keep trying until they get across. Economically, that's still their most
rational option. (in Dillon 2000, p. A4)

In this sense, the border patrol is simply a "speed bump" for the undocumented—but not for all of them. One undocumented immigrant who had been
turned back five times at the border began "hurling himself in front of traffic
in Agua Prieta. . . . After the police arrested him, he hung himself in his jail
cell" (Dillon 2000, p. A4).

In response to the INS crackdown on the undocumented, a *Denver Post*
editorial on January 3, 2000, criticized the stepped up campaign by arguing
that "undocumented foreigners are keeping our strong economy afloat." Their
solution was to "allow some Mexicans to work in the U.S. legally" (in Dillon
2000, p. A4). One border patrol supervisor, ensconced in his patrol car and
scanning the dark horizon for migrants through his infrared camera, sounded
philosophical: "You have to sympathize with these people. They're coming
from nothing, and they've got nothing to lose. They'll try again and again to
get across. I'd do the same thing if I were in their shoes" (Dillon 2000, p. A4).

In a third article in the *Boston Globe* written from the Los Angeles perspective, entitled "The Cost of Easy Living," the author quips that California's
welcome sign should read "Land of bargain-basement amenities" (Epstein
1997, p. E1). Every "trendy" restaurant has "cheap valet parking, there are
cheap car washes, cheap house cleaners, cheap manicures, cheap gardeners,
cheap nannies." Immigrant labor, often undocumented, provides "such sought-
after amenities for California's up-and-coming baby boomers." Why then
would these same Californians pass such an "anti-immigrant initiative as
Proposition 187, which [was] aimed at ending medical and education benefits for the children of undocumented aliens?"

The appalling answer is that Californians do not want to stop the flow of
foreign workers. "They just want to make sure that the costs remain low."
Economist Paul Krugman points out in the article that Proposition 187 was not
necessarily aimed at removing the undocumented. Krugman makes it clear that
"It simply says we will not spend any money on them, but an El Salvadoran can
still cut your grass even if his children are illiterate" (Epstein 1997, p. E5).

Krugman asserts that "California is a great place to be a tax lawyer or a high-tech executive, or consultant. I don't know if the benefits are very large for the average Anglo" (in Epstein 1997, p. E5).

Michael Peter Smith, a University of California professor who has studied "the fallout from Proposition 187," comments that

There's been no real pressure in California to enforce employer sanctions...It seems to me the climate is to have it both ways. Allow as much cheap labor into the country as possible, but at all costs don't reproduce any social welfare benefits...or even schooling. Let the Mexican Government . . . pick all that up. (in Epstein 1997, p. E5)

This article notes how easy it is "to control immigrant workers who have no legal standing" and ends with a vignette from a Los Angeles restaurant in which "the staff routinely plays a joke on new busboys by showing up in a kitchen wearing a hat with 'INS'—or Immigration and Naturalization Service—emblazoned on it. . . . It is a chilling glimpse of humor in the land of immigrant labor and a reminder that much of the cheap 'good life' comes at somebody's expense" (Epstein 1997, p. E5).

On August 30, 1999, the mayor of Douglas, Arizona, wrote an editorial for the *New York Times* entitled "Do You Hire Illegal Immigrants?" (p. A19). In this article, Mayor Borane describes his small desert city of Douglas, Arizona, a sister city to Agua Prieta, which is close to the Mexican border. He describes his town as inhabited by "working people, ranchers and fixed-income retirees," 95 percent of whom are Hispanic. And then he identifies his audience—to whom he is addressing his question—namely, those who live in the more "wealthy, enterprising and opulent places" in the nation. He writes about what these two quite diverse groups hold in common by asking one question: "Do you have any idea what havoc you cause in our area and in other border towns, all because some of you hire illegal immigrants to make your beds, mow your lawns and cook your meals?" (p. A19).

Since the beginning of 1999, in this small area the border patrol has apprehended and expelled 200,000 Mexican and Latin American immigrants, 60,500 in March alone. Many others make it through—"hungry, thirsty, and desperate." The mayor speaks of the negative impact of these waves of undocumented immigrants passing "through their property at night, cutting water lines and littering fields with plastic jugs, diapers and other trash" (Borane 1999, p. A19).

Mayor Borane goes on to list the "costs" of "winking at the law" by hiring large numbers of undocumented immigrants for their "homes, hotels, restaurants, landscaping businesses, fields, orchards, factories, construction crews and any other sector that exploits them" (p. A19). There are costs to the community when "property values and business opportunities are trampled because of the job pull you have created." There are costs to the undocumented in terms of "the arduous, debasing journey" they make, at the mercy of the elements, and

the "unscrupulous human traffickers," or "coyotes," who "stuff trusting individuals into vans in conditions intolerable for animals." INS agents and ranchers will sometimes find "men, women and children dead of heat exhaustion."

The editorial goes on to describe the process whereby compassion fatigue
sets in:

Compassion is reaching its limits in border areas like ours. Drained by the costs, both
public and private, and the risks posed by the migrants' desperation, some ranchers
and other citizens have taken up arms to protect their property. What they are doing is
wrong, but it is what your demand for cheap and unregulated services has driven
them to. (p. A19)

The solution to this crisis, according to the mayor, is to legalize this labor
force through a guest worker program. He anticipates the response of the
wealthy to this legalization program:

Too expensive, you say? Higher pay and social services will dry up demand and rob
many of the world's ambitious down trodden of the "opportunity" you give them?
Believe that if you want, but the next time you read about a child who died crossing
the Arizona Desert, ask yourself those questions again. (p. A19)

These stark stories of relentless border crossings into the United States in
the midst of massive INS efforts to turn them back underscores the economic
dynamic that is at play: Some Americans benefit from undocumented immigration and some are hurt. On the whole it is the wealthier businesses and
consumers that benefit while costs accrue to those on the lower end of the
economic ladder (Isbister, in Jonas and Thomas 1999, p. 85). If one were to
do a cost–benefit analysis or a "push–pull" analysis from the angle of the
undocumented, lining up the risks next to the opportunities, the benefits of
migration would outweigh the costs, because, for the most part, abject poverty and desperation are the starting points for the undocumented. Taking
advantage of the wretched plight of the undocumented for the sake of economic gain is a scar on the American conscience.

The legislative initiatives on undocumented immigration coupled with the
descriptive data gleaned from contemporary news headlines paints a picture
of a deteriorating environment for undocumented immigrants. The flickering
flame of concern about the human rights of the undocumented, voiced earlier
for the first time during IRCA's legislative debate in the late 1970s and early
1980s, had been dimmed during the 1990s and at the start of the new century.

DO THE UNDOCUMENTED HAVE HUMAN OR CIVIL RIGHTS?

After full implementation of IRCA, by all accounts, the undocumented did
not return to their countries of origin. Their plight in this country, as a result
of the implementation of IRCA, is at heart a human rights issue because it

touches on their right to work, to sustenance, and to legal recourse. Immigration scholar Vernon Briggs drives home the point that "in the U.S., the plight of illegal aliens is one of the most reprehensible aspects of contemporary America [*sic*] life." He recounts one congressional staff member observing that "nobody gives a damn" about undocumented immigrants because they are "nobody's constituents" (1984, p. 167). The basic human right that is at stake for the undocumented, despite their relatively insignificant numbers, is the right to life itself and therefore the right of "access to those things essential to support life" (Mahoney 1994, p. 88). From this proposition several questions full of legal and ethical knots arise. Do the undocumented have the right to pursue such basic necessities as education, health care, housing, and employment? Tomasi (1999) notes that "the best alternative that the young, daring poor possess [is] the option of movement" (p. 4). The 1952 Convention on Refugees asserted that the right to leave one's country is universal, but was silent on the right to enter another country: "Better silence than evident contradiction" (Sassen 1999, p. 16).

It can be argued that the undocumented should not be in the United States in the first place and that the IRCA legislation focused on preventing future undocumented immigration by "drying up" both the job market and most social services that might be available to them. This raises a key question: Do undocumented immigrants have human rights? The answer to this question, as with many issues surrounding the undocumented, is both yes and no. The U.S. Supreme Court has stated that the undocumented have protection under the Fifth and Fourteenth Amendments:

There are literally millions of aliens within the jurisdiction of the United States. The Fifth Amendment, as well as the Fourteenth Amendment, protects every one of these persons from deprivation of life, liberty or property without due process. . . . Even one whose presence in this country is unlawful, involuntary, or transitory, is entitled to that Constitutional protection. (Hull 1983, p. 227)

A dilemma exists however, if the undocumented cannot or will not claim these rights because of fear of deportation and separation from family, can they be said to actually have these rights? The first clause of the Fourteenth Amendment says, "[No state] shall deny to any person within its jurisdiction the equal protection of the law." It remains unclear to what extent, if any, this statute covers the undocumented (Hull 1983, p. 228).

Hull points out that the United States has been unwilling to ratify any human rights agreements that have binding legal claims in U.S. or international courts. Rather, ratification has been limited to agreements such as the Universal Declaration of Human Rights and the United Nations Charter that "lack the status of law and hence impose no international obligation." The one overriding reason for not ratifying legally binding human rights treaties is that the United States would thus relinquish some of its national sovereignty.

If legally binding agreements were signed, they would furnish the undocumented with an effective tool of redress in U.S. courts (1983, pp. 237–238).

As it stands, "The protection provided most undocumented aliens depends largely upon the prevailing values of the host countries and the political clout of the sending countries." In the dialogue on human rights, the United States has earned itself the reputation of hypocrisy by pointing "an accusing finger at other countries . . . but steadfastly avoiding any mechanisms for monitoring conditions in its own country" (Hull 1983, pp. 226, 237). The most disturbing negative pattern toward the undocumented that has emerged in the 1990s is the actual reduction in the rights that the undocumented possess, particularly in the light of the 1996 immigration law which in effect has eliminated judicial review prior to deportation for the undocumented.

From a policy perspective, the immigration debate continues to rest largely on national sovereignty and economic self-interest. It is not possible to lay claim to any prevailing value that would compel intervention on behalf of the undocumented over and against a host of competing and conflicting interest. Post–World War II universal documents on human rights use language that does not distinguish citizens from resident or undocumented aliens but speaks instead in inclusive language: "Everyone has a right to," or "No one shall be," indicating, as Hull points out, "that the specific right at issue inheres in every human being, irrespective of nationality" (1983, p. 230).

Sashia Sassen in her article "Beyond Sovereignty: Immigration Policy Making Today" points out the discrepancy that exists between nations of the world lifting "border controls for the flow of capital, information, and services" in order to make way for economic globalization and yet nations such as the United States, Japan, and those in Western Europe are still laying claim to older concepts of national sovereignty and control of their borders (in Jonas and Thomas 1999, p. 15). The idea that Sassen sets forth is that the notion of sovereignty itself will be transformed in the process of economic globalization through its "supranational organizations, international agreements on human rights, and the new emergent private international legal regime for business transactions" (1999, p. 15).

For the first time in history, we are witnessing a global flow of capital, information, and technology, which also implies that social problems will be globalized (Sassen 1999, p. 15). In this context, it may be that global human rights initiatives will finally begin to grapple with the daunting issue of genuine, unequivocal human rights for every human being, including undocumented immigrants.

THE GLOBAL CHALLENGE

Increasingly we live in a world of "porous borders and interconnected economies" due to the computer-driven revolution of the 1970s and the globalization of the economy into a single, worldwide market (Schmenann 1999, p. 1).

Friedman (1999) in his groundbreaking book on globalization, *The Lexus and the Olive Tree*, speaks of globalization as a process of integrating markets, nation-states, and technologies into a dynamic, worldwide system that allows "individuals, corporations and nation-states to reach around the world farther, faster, deeper and cheaper than ever before." However, globalization is also "producing a powerful backlash for those brutalized or left behind by the new system." If the Internet is the main symbol of the era of globalization indicative of our interconnectedness, it also signals a sense that "nobody is in charge" (1999, pp. 7, 8, 11). As multinational corporations have gained in economic and political power, the nation-states or individual countries are getting weaker and weaker in their ability to organize their own economies. This is particularly the case in Third World countries where crippling indebtedness to First World countries make economic development impossible because these countries cannot afford the new technology. If this pattern persists, the massive migrations of people from poor countries to richer countries can be predicted well into the twenty-first century (Sampeo 1997). Currently, one-third of humanity still remains below the poverty level. The continued growing gap between rich and poor countries will provide the impetus or push factor for continued migration. As a free-lance writer from Portland, Maine, has ominously warned with pithy clarity, "If bread is not brought to the people, the people will come to the bread" (Dinn 1997).

Nestor Rodriguez in his article "The Battle for the Borders: Notes on Autonomous Migration, Trans-National Communities and the State" painted a fascinating if not surreal picture of the global landscape on the cusp of the twenty-first century. He describes the movement of "billions of capital investment dollars" across world regions and millions of migrant peoples moving across the global expanse of the nation-states (1999, p. 27).

Economic agreements such as NAFTA, EC, and GATT have helped to move transnational capital on a worldwide scale, unencumbered by government restrictions or local control. However, it is the dynamism and the independence of the human movement of one hundred million people relocating across the borders of countries in "Eastern and Western Europe, Asia, Africa, Latin America, the Caribbean, and North America" that is the more astonishing phenomenon (Rodriguez 1999, p. 27).

It is mesmerizing because it is an "autonomous" movement of "working-class" and "peasant communities" in developing countries crossing the borders of other nation-states for the purpose of survival. The point to be taken from his description is that thus far the only "fixed value" that is considered in the debate on undocumented immigration is what benefits the nation-states in terms of the "national interest" and not what may be of concern to undocumented immigrants collectively "or humankind in general." For Rodriguez, the battle for the U.S.–Mexican border in the 1990s through increased border agents, the erection of fences, walls, and ditches, and the attempts to deny education for U.S.–born children of the undocumented, was actually an attempt to control "Autonomous Migration." What Rodriguez means by au-tonomous international migration is the movement of workers, their families, and communities without state regulation or intergovernment agreements. He calls it a "state-free migration" (1999, pp. 28, 29, 40).

In all this, Rodriguez points out that the struggle is to "maintain nation-state borders in a global context made increasingly fluid by the heightened transnational migration of capital and labor." It is also about the "changing significance of nation-states" and their national boundaries in the new global order. Rodriguez suggests that the battle for the U.S. border will ultimately be lost because autonomous migration from peripheral countries is a "worker-led transnational socio-spacial reconfiguration"—that is, it is an attempt by working-class communities from developing countries "to spacially reorga-nize their base of social reproduction in the global landscape." Just as the late twentieth century had seen capital expand globally in search of new resources, so also have working-class communities from developing countries sought to expand "their base of survival" through autonomous, undocumented immi-gration (Rodriguez 1999, pp. 28, 29, 39).

Rodriguez points out that if all of this seems "farfetched," it might be be-cause this new phenomenon explodes existing social science conceptual cat-egories. This means that there is need to move beyond "the use of the individual as the unit of analysis" to the broader patterns of "transnational changes in a post-national era." The threat to the nation-states that undocumented immi-gration poses lies not in illegal immigration as such, but its autonomous na-ture. By way of example, Rodriguez points out then Governor Pete Wilson's visit to Congress in the aftermath of passage of Proposition 187, which had for its purpose the promotion of a new "*bracero* migrant program." Clearly, the battle for the border is not about ending undocumented immigration, but about "terminating its autonomous origin" (1999, pp. 39, 40).

THE DEBT TRAP

Throughout this book allusion has been made to the fact that in national and congressional debate on undocumented immigration, insufficient atten-tion was paid to the push factors that propel the undocumented to migrate from their countries of origin. In order to examine one overriding push fac-tor—that of grinding, unrelenting, large-scale poverty—the problem of in-debtedness of poor, underdeveloped countries to wealthier, industrialized nations needs to be explicated because it is often debt repayment that pre-vents poor countries from making progress in basic development such as edu-cation, medicine, communications technology, and other means of alleviating poverty. Many poor countries are struggling to pay the interest on their debt without making any dent on the loan itself. When 40 percent of the annual budget of countries is going toward debt reduction, there can be few resources left for poverty reduction efforts. This situation has been compounded over the last twenty years because of serious cutbacks in foreign aid packages ("Poor Nations and the Debt Trap" 1999, p. A30).

In the 1970s in particular, when interest rates were low, poor countries were encouraged by major lenders such as the World Bank to apply for loans. With little regulation, much of this money was squandered through mismanagement or misguided priorities; in some instances, it was simply spirited away into private bank accounts ("Poor Nations and the Debt Trap" 1999, p. A30). One of the abiding obstacles erected by poor, underdeveloped countries that has been difficult to surmount in the external debt debate has been Third World countries' unrealistic claim to national sovereignty in using "government expenditures as they see fit" (Powers 1999, p. A23). Gradually, as Powers has explained, poor countries have learned that they cannot say, "We have a sound macro economic plan; economic growth will lift all boats. Give us the money." This claim on national sovereignty has gradually shifted, giving way to the idea that "debt relief must be tied directly to poverty reduction schemes," such as education for the girl child, health care, and clean drinking water (Powers 1999, p. A23).

In an editorial in the *Boston Globe* entitled "Selfish Charity," the author indicated that the World Bank together with the International Monetary Fund (IMF) and other leading lending institutions had identified forty-one of the countries where indebtedness has reached in the aggregate $170 billion. The point is made that addressing the debt problem is not all altruism from the perspective of wealthier countries. Indebted, poor countries sell their own basic commodities such as minerals and other raw materials at "whatever price they can get." In turn, this not only drives down their own income, but it is borne, as usual, "on the backs of those people at the bottom of the economic pile." When debt repayment cripples poor countries in their attempt to alleviate poverty through basic development, it also curtails their ability "to become better customers" in the marketplace for the products of the developed countries. The author makes the point that "breaking this chain" is complex, not easily solved and expensive—but "the alternative is, in the long run, far more costly" ("Selfish Charity" 1999, p. A18). Among the costs absorbed by wealthier nations is the largely unwelcome human stream of millions of undocumented immigrants winding their way toward healthier economies.

The debt relief issue has risen to the top of the agenda at the United Nations and international monetary meetings due to "the diligent, long-term activism of numerous nongovernmental, religious and union groups that have been working on [this issue] for decades." At the "Group of Eight" meeting in Cologne, Germany, in June 1999, the leaders of the seven major industrialized nations plus Russia opened their meeting by asserting that "debt relief for the poorest nations is, after Kosovo, the most significant item on the international agenda" (Powers 1999 p. A23). The seven wealthiest nations entered into an agreement, dubbed the "Cologne Initiative," "that could eliminate up to $90 billion in debts owed by nearly three dozen impoverished countries". This debt relief was tied to three goals: education, health care, and AIDS prevention. Touted as "a humane effort to promote widely shared prosperity in the new millennium," it fell far short of the $170 billion owed by the poorest forty-one countries, but it was a step in the right direction (Babington 1999, pp. F1, F2).

In issuing its development report in July 1999, the United Nations noted that "globalization is compounding the gap between rich and poor nations and intensifying American dominance of the world's economic and cultural markets. . . . The reports warn that the glaring, growing inequalities in the distribution of wealth pose a 'dangerous polarization' between rich and poor countries" (Miller 1999, p. A8). Quoting from Mandela, the same report highlights the unequal and inequitable distribution of wealth by noting that

The top fifth of countries had eighty six percent of the Gross Domestic Product (GDP); the bottom fifth just one percent. The top fifth command eighty-two percent of the world export markets and sixty eight percent of foreign direct investment; the bottom fifth had just one percent of each of these. (2000, p. A15)

The U.N. report also noted the enormous gap that exists between "globally well-connected" and "unconnected" peoples in terms of the Internet. For example, "an American needs to save a month's salary to buy a computer; a Bangladeshi must save all of his wages for eight years to do so." The British Economist who authored the U.N. report asserts that it is "neither anti-American nor anti-free market." He notes that the report endorses markets "as the best guarantee of efficiency but not necessarily of equity" (Mandela 2000, p. A8).

In our new globalized world environment, countries are quickly learning that "the economic fate of a country is not solely in its own hands." Events in far off places can have immense consequences on the financial well-being of countries not at all involved in the event in question. This realization that the nations of the world effect one another's economic fate should heighten our awareness that "a simple reliance on the market to eradicate poverty and gross inequality is a grave fallacy. . . . We all know that the market with all its benefits does not, as it were, sort it all out" (Mandela 2000, p. A15).

Kofi Annan, secretary-general of the United Nations, reflecting on the failure of the World Trade Organization's meeting in Seattle, faulted the world's leading economic powers for putting in place trade barriers that are "helping to exclude developing nations from the benefits of global trade." In calling for a "Global New Deal," Annan challenges industrialized countries "to spread the advantages of the freer flow of goods, jobs and capital among all countries that are open to investment" (2000, p. 12). Thus far globalization has spread its economic bounty to certain select "groups of people, countries and corporations," while other peoples and nations are being cast backwards into more primitive levels of development. As long as the rewards and opportunities of globalization are this skewed, the most fundamental global challenge in the third millennium will be the eradication of a sea of large-scale poverty in the midst of small islands of concentrated wealth and opulence (Mandela 2000, p. A15).

The interrelated problems of the "debt trap," the ever-widening gap between rich and poor countries, and the backlash of economic globalization on poor countries provide, in broad strokes, an explanatory context for looking at how Third World poverty has become an overriding push factor in the global migration of people. "The increasing movement of people on a global scale is a new phenomenon in the history of our world" (Bacon 1999, p. 172). As noted earlier by Nester Rodriquez, there is a discernable parallel between the "movement across world regions of billions of capital investment dollars" and the growth of worldwide migration of the economically dispossessed (1999, p. 27).

Undocumented immigration is a global social problem that needs global solutions that are based on binding human rights agreements for all persons in all circumstances and economic development plans that create greater equity for the poor in all countries.

America must reckon with its historic ambivalence toward undocumented immigrants, whereby we place them in a subservient status for economic gain and at the same time hold fast to "deep convictions about the equality of all people" (Isbister, in Jonas and Thomas 1999, p. 85). America can continue its local, myopic, isolated, residual, and often mean-spirited attempts to stave off the human flow of undocumented immigrants at its back door, or it can join comprehensive global efforts at reordering economic priorities so that poor countries, who are the source of undocumented immigration, will be able to sustain the poor in their own home countries, thus sparing them and the world their sad odyssey across the global landscape.

References

Abrams, F. S. "American Immigration Policy: How Strait the Gate?" In *U.S. Immigration Policy*, edited by R. R. Hofstetter. Durham, N.C.: Duke University Press, 1984.

Ainsworth, R. G. *Illegal Immigrants and Refugees: Their Economic Adaptation and Impact on Local U.S. Labor Markets*. Washington, D.C.: National Commission for Employment Policy, 1986.

Annan, K. "U.N. Chief Blames Rich Nations for Failure of Trade Talks." Bangkok, Thailand. *New York Times*, February 13, 2000, pp. 12, A15.

Anzovin, S., ed. *The Problem of Immigration*. New York: H. W. Wilson, 1985.

Babington, C. "G-7 Offers Aid to Poor Nations." *Boston Globe*, June 19, 1999, pp. F1, F2.

Bach, R. "The Process of Immigration Reform." In *Defense of the Alien*, vol. 21, edited by L. F. Tomasi. New York: Center for Migration Studies, 1999.

Bacon, D. "For an Immigration Policy Based on Human Rights." In *Immigration: A Civil Rights Issue for the Americas*, edited by S. Jonas and S. D. Thomas. Wilmington, Del.: Scholarly Resources, 1999.

Bean, F. D., J. Schmandt, and S. Weintraub. *Mexican and Central American Population and U.S. Immigration Policy*. Austin: University of Texas, 1989.

Borane, R. "Do You Hire Illegal Immigrants?" *New York Times*, August 30, 1999, p. A19.

Bowsher, C. *Immigration Reform: Employer Sanctions and the Question of Discrimination*. Washington, D.C.: U. S. Government Printing Office, March 1990.

Briggs, V. M. *Immigration Policy and the American Labor Force.* Baltimore: Johns Hopkins University Press, 1984.

————. "The Albatross of Immigration Reform: Temporary Worker Policy in the United States." *International Migration Review* 20, no. 4 (1987): 995–1017.

Brimelow, P. *Alien Nation: Common Sense about America's Immigration Disaster.* New York: Random House, 1995.

Bryce-Laporte, R. S. "The New Immigration: Its Origin, Visibility, and Implications for Public Policy." In *Ethnicity and Race,* edited by W. A. VanHorne. Milwaukee: American Ethnic Studies, 1982.

"California Indicts the Immigration Law." *America* 162, no. 7. (1990): 163.

Carrasco, G. P. "The Golden Moment of Legalization." *Migration and Refugee Services.* United States Catholic Conference, Washington, D.C., 1987.

Chiswick, B. R. "Immigration Policy and the National Interest." In U.S. Immigration Policy and the National Interest, Staff Report of the Select Commission on Immigration and Refugee Policy (SCIRP). Washington, D.C., April 30, 1981.

————. *The Gateway: U.S. Immigration Issues and Policies.* Washington, D.C.: American Enterprise Institute for Public Policy Research, 1982.

Cockroft, J. D. *Outlaws in the Promised Land.* New York: Grove Press, 1986.

Cose, E. *A Nation of Strangers.* New York: William Morrow, 1992.

Crewdson, J. *The Tarnished Door.* New York: Times Books, 1983.

Dillon, S. "Boom Turns Border into Speed Bump." *New York Times,* January 18, 2000, p. A4.

Dinn, J. "If bread is not brought to the people, the people will go to the bread." Freelance writer, Portland, 1997.

"Doors and Walls" (editorial). *America,* April 11, 1987, p. 274.

Ehrenberg, R. G., and R. S. Smith. *Modern Labor Economics, Theory and Public Policy.* Boston: Scott, Foresman, 1982.

Epstein, E. "The Cost of Easy Living." *Boston Globe,* May 11, 1997, pp. E1, E5.

Espenshade, T. J., J. L. Baraka, and G. A Huber. "Immigration Reform, Welfare Reform and Future Patterns of U.S. Immigration." In *In Defense of the Alien,* vol. 21, edited by L. F. Tomasi. New York: Center for Migration Studies, 1999.

Firestone, D. "Guiliani Criticizes a U.S. Crackdown on Illegal Aliens." *New York Times,* August 23, 1995, pp. 1, 1A.

Fogel, W. "Nonimmigrant Labor Policy: Future Trend or Aberration?" In *The Unavoidable Issue,* edited by D. G. Papademetriou and M. J. Miller. Philadelphia: Institute for the Study of Human Issues, 1983.

Foner, N. *New Immigrants in New York.* New York: Columbia Press, 1987.

Forbes, S. S. "Doing Well by Doing Good: The Impact of Legal Immigration on the United States." In T. Hesburgh, U.S. Immigration Policy and the National Interest, Staff Report of the Select Commission on Immigration and Refugee Policy (SCIRP). Washington, D.C., April 30, 1981.

Friedman, T. L. *The Lexus and the Olive Tree.* New York: Farrar, Straus, Giroux, 1999.

Fuch, L., and S. Forbes. "Immigration and U.S. History: The Evolution of the Open Society." In T. Hesburgh, U.S. Immigration Policy and the National Interest, Staff Report of the Select Commission on Immigration and Refugee Policy (SCIRP). Washington, D.C., April 30, 1981.

Fuchs, L. H. "First Principles of Immigration Reform: The Open Society." In U.S. Immigration Policy and the National Interest, Staff Report of the Select Commission on Immigration and Refugee Policy (SCIRP). Washington, D.C., April 30, 1981

————. "The Search for a Sound Immigration Policy: A Personal View." In *Clamor at the Gates*, edited by N. Glazer. San Francisco: Institute for Contemporary Studies, 1985.

————. *The American Kaleidoscope: Race, Ethnicity and Civil Culture*. Hanover, N.H.: Wesleyan University Press, 1990.

————. Review of *A Nation of Strangers*, by Ellis Cose. *Boston Globe*, March 29, 1992.

Gelfand, D. E., and R. Bialik-Gilad. "Immigration Reform and Social Work." *Social Work: Journal of the National Association of Social Workers* 34 no. 1 (January 1989): 23.

Gimpel, J. G., and J. R. Edwards, Jr. *The Congressional Politics of Immigration Reform*. Boston: Allyn and Bacon, 1999.

Glazer, N. *Clamor at the Gates*. San Francisco: Institute for Contemporary Studies, 1985.

"Glowing Dust Urged for Use at U.S. Borders." Reprinted in the *Boston Globe* from the Associated Press, August 27, 1994.

Gordenker, L. "Immigration Reform: The United States and Western Europe." In *The Unavoidable Issue*, edited by D. G. Papademetriou and M. J. Miller. Philadelphia: Institute for the Study of Human Issues, 1983.

Gordon, J. Unpublished testimony before Boston City Council. Boston, Mass., March 1988.

Havemann, J. "Suit Challenges Welfare Laws." *Boston Globe*, March 27, 1999 (from *The Washington Post*).

Heilberger, M. *Statement on Behalf of Massachusetts Immigrants*. Unpublished testimony before the Boston City Council. Boston, Mass., 1988.

Heilberger, M., F. Adieli, and M. Fried. *Keeping the Promise?* A report on the Legalization Program of the Immigration Reform and Control Act of 1986: Massachusetts at the Halfway Mark. Boston: Massachusetts Immigration and Refugee Advocacy Group, November 5, 1987.

Hesburgh, T. U.S. Immigration Policy and the National Interest, Staff Report of the Select Commission on Immigration and Refugee Policy (SCIRP). Washington, D.C., April 30, 1981.

Hesburgh, T. U.S. Immigration Policy and the National Interest, Final Report of the Select Commission on Immigration and Refugee Policy (SCIRP). Washington, D.C., March 1, 1981.

Hoefer, M. Commonwealth of Massachusetts, in a letter to author from Regina Lee, from Executive Office of Human Resource, INS Statistics. Boston, July 27, 1992.

Hofstetter, R. R., ed. *U.S. Immigration Policy*. Durham, N.C.: Duke University Press, 1984.

Hull, E. "The Rights of Aliens: National and International Issue." In *The Unavoidable Issue*, edited by D. G. Papademetriou and M. J. Miller. Philadelphia: Institute for the Study of Human Issues, 1983.

Isbister, J. "Are Immigration Controls Ethical?" In *Immigration: A Civil Rights Issue for the Americas*, edited by S. Jonas and S. D. Thomas. Wilmington: Scholarly Resources, 1999.

Johnson, D. Unpublished proposal, Haitian Multi-Service Center. Boston, Mass., 1987.

Johnston, D. C. "Gap between Rich and Poor Found Substantially Wider." *New York Times*, September 5, 1999, p. 14.

Jonas, S., and S. D. Thomas, eds. *Immigration: A Civil Rights Issue for the Americas*. Wilmington: Scholarly Resources, 1999.

Keeley, C. "Population and Immigration Policy: State and Federal Roles." In *Mexican and Central American Population and U.S. Immigration Policy*, edited by F. D. Bean, J. Schmandt, and S. Weintraub. Austin: Center for Mexican American Studies, University of Texas at Austin, 1989.

Leen, H. "New Irish Immigrants." *Boston Pilot*, March 3, 1989, pp. 1, 8.

LeMay, M. C. *From Open Door to Dutch Door: An Analysis of Immigration Policy since 1820*. New York: Praeger, 1987.

———. *Anatomy of a Public Policy: The Reform of Contemporary American Immigration Law*. Westport, Conn.: Praeger, 1994.

Lewis, A. "With Exquisite Cruelty." *New York Times*, February 28, 1997, p. A35.

Light, P. *Artful Work: The Politics of Social Security Reform*. New York: Random House, 1985.

Mahoney, R. "Immigration Policy: Seven Guiding Principles." *Origins* 23, no. 33 (February 3, 1994): 88.

Majchrzak, A. *Methods for Policy Research*. Beverly Hills, Calif.: Sage, 1984.

Mandela, N. "Globalizing Responsibility." *Boston Globe*, January 4, 2000.

Mayer, R. R. *Policy and Program Planning: A Developmental Perspective*. Englewood Cliffs, N.J.: Prentice Hall, 1985.

Meissner, D. M., and D. G. Papademetriou. *The Legalization of Undocumented Aliens: A Third Quarter Assessment*. Washington, D.C.: The Carnegie Endowment for International Peace, 1988.

Meissner, D. M., D. G. Papademetriou, and D. S. North. *Legalization of Undocumented Aliens: Lessons from Other Countries* (monograph). Washington, D.C.: The Carnegie Endowment for International Peace, 1986.

Midgley, E. "Comings and Goings in U.S. Immigration Policy." In *The Unavoidable Issue*, edited by D. G. Papademetriou and M. J. Miller. Philadelphia: Institute for the Study of Human Issues, 1983.

Miller, J. "Globalization Widens Rich–Poor Gap, U.N. Report Says." *New York Times*, July 13, 1999, p. A8.

Moore, R. J. *A New Immigration Policy?: Problems and Prospects* (book review). Princeton, N.J.: Woodrow Wilson School, Princeton University, 1985, p. 613.

Morris, M. D. *Immigration: The Beleaguered Bureaucracy*. Washington, D.C.: The Brookings Institution, 1985.

Nieves, E. "California Initiative Denying Services to Illegal Aliens Is Killed." *New York Times*, July 30, 1999, pp. 1, A15.

North, D. S., and A. M. Portes. *Through the Maze: An Interim Report on the Alien Legalization Program*. Washington, D.C.: Trans Century Development Associates, 1988.

Ocasio, L. "The Year of the Immigrant as Scapegoat." *Report on the Americas* 29, no. 3 (November–December 1995): p. 17.

"One U.S. Resident in 10 Is Now Foreign Born." *New York Times*, September 17, 1999, p. 37.

Papademetriou, D. G., and M. J. Miller, eds. *The Unavoidable Issue*. Philadelphia: Institute for the Study of Human Issues, 1983.

Papademetriou, D. G., and N. DiMarzio. *Undocumented Aliens in the New York Metropolitan Area*. New York: Center for Migration Studies, 1986.

Pedraza-Bailey, S. *Political and Economic Migrants in America: Cubans and Mexicans*. Austin: University of Texas Press, 1985.

Perales, C. A. *The Immigration Reform and Control Act of 1986: New York's Response*. Albany: New York State Inter-Agency Task Force on Immigration Affairs, 1987.

Piore, M. J. *Birds of Passage*. New York: Hamilton Printing Press, 1979.

"Poor Nations and the Death Trap" (editorial). *New York Times*, April 30, 1999, p. A30.

Portes, A. M., and D. A. Kincaid. "Alternative Outcomes of Reform." *Society* (May–June 1985): 73, 74, 90.

Powers, J. "A Global Easing of Rich and Poor Rift." *Boston Globe*, June 21, 1999, p. A23.

Reimers, D. M. "Recent Immigration Policy: An Analysis." In *The Gateway U.S. Immigration Issues and Policies*, edited by B. R. Cheswick. Washington, D.C.: American Enterprise Institute, 1982.

————. *Still the Golden Door*. New York: Columbia University Press, 1985.

Rodriguez, N. "The Battle for the Borders: Notes on Autonomous Migration, Trans-National Communities and the State." In *Immigration: A Civil Rights Issue for the Americas*, edited by S. Jonas and S. D. Thomas. Wilmington: Scholarly Resources, 1999.

Roney, L. "The Present Immigration System: Its Origins and Operation." In T. Hesburgh, U.S. Immigration Policy and the National Interest, Staff Report of the Select Commission on Immigration and Refugee Policy (SCIRP). Washington, D.C., April 30, 1981.

Sampeo, P. "Globalization of the Economy and Its Impact on Developing Countries." International Conference on Globalization, Angers, France, 1997.

Sassen, S. "Beyond Sovereignty: Immigration Policy Making Today." In *Immigration: A Civil Rights Issue for the Americas*, edited by S. Jonas and S. D. Thomas. Wilmington: Delaware: Scholarly Resources, 1999.

Schmenann, S. "What's Wrong with This Picture of Nationalism?" *New York Times*, February 21, 1999, p. 1.

Schmitt, E. "Illegal Immigrants Rose to 5 Million in '96." *New York Times*, February 8, 1997, p. 9.

Seiber, C. *City of Somerville Minority and Immigrant Needs Assessment*. Cambridge, Mass.: Prospect Associates, 1988.

"Selfish Charity" (editorial). *Boston Globe*, June 19, 1999, p. A18.

Seller, M. S. "Historical Perceptives on American Immigration Policy: Case Studies and Current Implications." In *U.S. Immigration Policy*, edited by R. R. Hofstetter. Durham, N.C.: Duke University Press, 1984.

Simcox, E. E., ed. *U.S. Immigration in the 1980s*. Washington, D.C.: Westview Press, 1988.

Simon, J. L. *The Economic Consequences of Immigration*. Cambridge: Blackwell, 1989.

Stone, E. *The Impact of the Immigration Reform and Control Act of 1986 in Massa-chusetts*. Unpublished document. Brandeis University and MIRA, Waltham, 1989.

"Sweatshops Are Returning to America." *People*, June 10, 1996.

Tomasi, L. "The Immigration and Nationality Act Must Be Amended by Congress." *Immigration World* 27, nos. 1–2 (November 1, 1999): 4.

U.S. Commission on Civil Rights. *The Tarnished Golden Door*. Washington, D.C.: The Commission, September 1980.

Verhovek, S. H. "Silent Deaths Climbing Steadily as Migrants Cross Mexican Bor-ders." *New York Times*, August 24, 1997, p. 1.

Williams, W. *The Implementation Perspective: A Guide for Managing Social Service Delivery Programs*. Berkeley and Los Angeles: University of California Press, 1980.

Williamson, C. *American's False Conscience: The Immigration Mystique*. New York: Basic Books, 1996.

Index

ABOUT THE AUTHOR

Helene Hayes is Chief Administrator of the New York, New Jersey, and Massachusetts division of the Good Shepherd Sisters, an international congregation of women religious. Dr. Hayes has served as Executive Director of a Haitian Multi-Service Center in Boston and has been an Instructor at the Boston University Continuing Education program. As an Adjunct Assistant Professor at Boston University Graduate School of Social Work and an Instructor at Boston College Graduate School of Social Work, Dr. Hayes has taught social policy analysis and the social welfare system.